The ABC of Palmistry

Also from Westphalia Press
westphaliapress.org

The ABC of Palmistry

Character and Fortune Revealed

by Well-Known Palmist

WESTPHALIA PRESS

An Imprint of Policy Studies Organization

Westphalia Press
An imprint of Policy Studies Organization
1527 New Hampshire Ave., NW
Washington, D.C. 20036
info@ipsonet.org

ISBN-13: 978-1-63391-610-4
ISBN-10: 1-63391-610-3

Cover design by Jeffrey Barnes:
jbarnesbook.design

Daniel Gutierrez-Sandoval, Executive Director
PSO and Westphalia Press

Updated material and comments on this edition
can be found at the Westphalia Press website:
www.westphaliapress.org

THE
A B C
OF
PALMISTRY,

TO ALL WHO WOULD PLAY

BRIDGE

THE

A B C OF BRIDGE

BY

E. A. TENNANT

IS THE BOOK YOU WANT

Rules of the Game, How to Score, What to Lead,
and How to Play

IN RED CLOTH, WHITE LETTERING

Price ONE SHILLING

PRESS NOTICES

Saturday Review.—" We have not met a better guide."

The Onlooker.—" We commend this shilling's worth to all beginners as
a genuinely gilt-edged investment."

*This book will be found invaluable to all entering
Bridge Competitions*

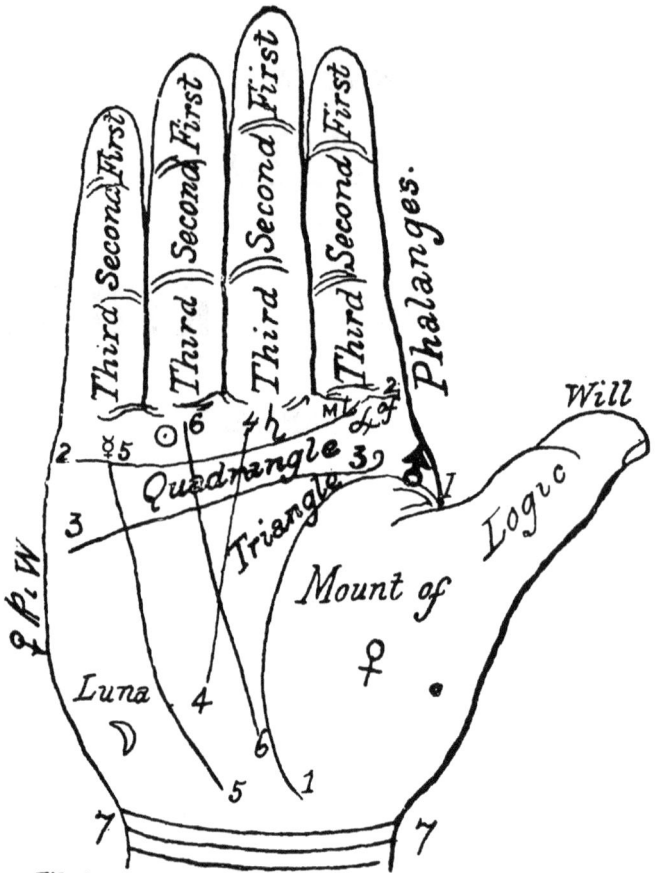

Third Second First
Third Second First
Third Second First
Third Second First

Phalanges.

Will

Quadrangle

Triangle

Mount of Logic

☿♄W

Luna ☽

Mount of ♀

1 Vital
2 Mensal
3 Cerebral
4 Saturnian
5 Hepatica
6 Solar

7 The Rascette

THE A B C ❧

❧ ❧ ❧ ❧ OF

PALMISTRY. ❧

CHARACTER AND FORTUNE REVEALED.

BY A WELL-KNOWN PALMIST. ❧

❧ WITH 12 FULL-PAGE ILLUSTRATIONS.

LONDON	NEW YORK
HENRY J. DRANE	WYCIL & COMPANY
SALISBURY HOUSE	PUBLISHERS
SALISBURY SQUARE	83 NASSAU STREET
FLEET STREET, E.C.	

DRANE'S NEW A B C HANDBOOKS

("AS EASY AS A B C")

A new series of small, attractively printed and bound volumes which will go in the pocket. Written by *Specialists*, they will be found to contain all worth knowing about the different subjects upon which they treat, and yet so clearly and plainly written that all who read will understand.

PRICE ONE SHILLING EACH.

The **A B C of Bridge**. By E. A. TENNANT. Description and Rules of the Game. How to Score. How to Play. What to Lead, &c., &c.

The **A B C of Photography**. By E. J. WALL. F.R.P.S.

The **A B C of Palmistry**; or, Character and Fortune Revealed by the Reading of the Hand. With twelve full-page illustrations.

The **A B C of Physiognomy**; or, How to Tell your Neighbour's Character by Reading His or Her Face. With six illustrations.

The **A B C of Graphology**. A Dictionary of Handwriting and Character. By WENTWORTH BENNET. With 170 illustrations

The **A B C of Dancing**. A Book of useful information and genuine Hints for Dancers and Learners. By EDWARD SCOTT.

The **A B C of Solo Whist**. By EDWIN OLIVER. Description and Rules of the Game. How to Score. What to Lead, &c.

The **A B C of Invalid Cookery**. By Mrs KIDDLE.

The **A B C of Carpentry**. By GEO. DAY.

The **A B C of the Horse**. By HAROLD TREMAYNE.

The **A B C of the Dog**. By HAROLD TREMAYNE.

The **A B C of Stamp Collecting**. By F. J. MELVILLE.

The **A B C Medical Guide**. By ALEXANDER AMBROSE, M.D.

The **A B C of Golf**. By A. J. ROBERTSON. Contains Full Instructions for Playing the Game, and complete List of Rules. Illustrated.

The **A B C of Physical Culture**. By ARTHUR RANSOME.

The **A B C of Phrenology**. By R. DIMSDALE STOCKER. Illustrated.

The **A B C of Chess**. Illustrated.

The **A B C of How to Speak Well**. By CHARLES HARTLEY.

The **A B C of Common Blunders**. By CHARLES HARTLEY.

The **A B C of Housekeeping**. A Guide to all Housekeepers. By J. N. BELL.

The **A B C of Swimming**. This book will teach anyone who can read how to Swim in Five minutes. By an Ex-Captain.

The **A B C of Gardening**. By a Practical Gardener.

The **A B C of Motoring**. By C. W. BROWN.

The **A B C of Bird Keeping**. By PERCIVAL W. WESTELL.

CONTENTS.

—o—

LIST OF ILLUSTRATIONS.

—o—

PREFATORY NOTE.

"All objections against a certain truth are in reality only negative evidence. 'We never observed this, we never experienced that.' Though ten thousand should make this assertion, what would it prove against one man of understanding and sound sense who would answer, 'But I have observed, and you also may observe if you please.'"—LAVATER.

It is with the hope of simplifying the complicated study of Palmistry that I offer this little book to the public. Although many others have written ably on this subject, no such book of reference has yet been published. As far as Palmistry is concerned I would say to those who choose to regard it with contempt what Galileo replied to the inquisitor who declared, with equal reason, that the earth remained stationary: "E pur si muove." To those who are open to conviction and would gladly believe I would say, "Come and see." Select any one characteristic sign and see if it be not confirmed in the hands of such persons as you know possess the quality indicated. This is a sceptical age, and perhaps the poet had reason when he wrote :—

> " This is all the gain
> We reap from all the wisdom sown
> Through ages. Nothing doubted those first sons
> Of time, while we, the schooled of centuries,
> Nothing believe."

But despite the general sceptical tone that characterizes modern thought, the majority are now ready to admit that the science of Physiognomy is based on proven facts, and is no idle claim of visionary brains. The only safe guide in life is common sense—the practical insight into things which are of instant and constant use to man—and every effect may be traced to a cause. It must be borne in mind that Nature is one, and that it is therefore most important when delineating character, either by Palmistry, Graphology, or Physiognomy, not to permit a person's manner or actions to explain away their real character. Charles Dickens, the great connoisseur of human nature, said truly, "We are all natural physiognomists; our fault lies in not heeding our instincts and first impressions sufficiently *by allowing people to come too near us and by their false actions explain away their real character."* Or in the words of Crabbe :—

> " It is the soul that sees.
> The outward eye presents the object.
> But the mind descries, and thence
> Delight, disgust, or cool indifference rise."

One must bear in mind that the sciences of Palmistry and Physiognomy often disclose traits and qualities which lie latent in the disposition, and which the force of circumstances may never have called into action. How often do we hear people say, " I never could have believed such a thing of Mrs. ——— or Mrs. ———. I never thought they were capable of that ! " But let no one here exclaim, " Then if I am born with an unfortunate character, an evil disposition, it is not my fault—I cannot help myself." With a strong will and a steady determination, no man is doomed to be a slave to any instincts or passions. The only fault that can never be overcome is weakness of character. Strength to resist is never wanting where a firm purpose is conceived, and it is only an idle pretext, a desire to excuse ourselves, that leads us to declare anything impossible. And again : people are often blamed for changeableness, but what makes us changeable in our friendships is the diffi- culty of discovering the qualities of the soul though it may be easy to know the characteristics of the mind. This difficulty is removed by the study of Palmistry and Physiognomy. For the sake of brevity, I have referred to the different lines by their Latin designations.

INTRODUCTION.

Iᴛ is worthy of notice that not only is the hand divided into three sections, the Divine, the Natural, and the Material, or the Spiritual, the Physical, and the Sensual, but that the fingers are also subject to these divisions. According as the Soul, Mind, or Body of the subject dominate, so will these sections be more or less developed. The upper part of the hand, comprising

The Mount of ♃ = Jupiter.
The Mount of ♄ = Saturn.
The Mount of ☉ = Apollo.
The Mount of ☿ = Mercury.
The Mount of ♂ = Mars.

and bounded by the Line of Heart or Mensal, is the divine portion; the Plain of Mars bounded by the Line of Head or Cerebral, the Natural, and the third

phalange of the thumb or Mount of Venus, in con-
junction with the Mount of Luna, the Material. The
same holds good with regard to the fingers, the upper
phalange representing the Spiritual, the second
phalange the Physical, and the third phalange the
Material. Each individual finger bears its own
import :—

The Thumb or Pollex = Will Power.
Finger of ♃ or Index = Power.
Finger of ♄ or Medius = Fatality.
Finger of ☉ or Annularis = Light.
Finger of ☿ or Auricularis = Science.

Or, again, the hand has been divided into two great
divisions, the Upper, or Masculine, containing such
Mounts as express Strength and Force, including the
Plain of Mars, and the Lower, or Feminine, including
the Mounts of Venus ♀ and Luna ☽. The shape
and consistency of the hands must be duly considered
since Chirognomy and Chiromancy are indissolubly
connected. In conclusion I would say with Lavater,
" The grand secret of simplifying science consists in
analyzing, in beginning with what is easy and proceeding progressively. The mountain of knowledge must
be climbed step by step."

VOCABULARY OF TERMS.

The finger of Jupiter ♃, or first finger, with the Mount beneath it.

The finger of Saturn ♄, or second finger, with the Mount beneath.

The finger of Apollo ☉, or third finger, with the Mount beneath.

The finger of Mercury ☿, or fourth finger, with the Mount beneath.

The First Phalange is that portion of the finger which bears the nail.

The Second Phalange is that portion of the finger lying between the first and second joints.

The Third Phalange is that portion of the finger which is found between the second and third joints.

The Knot of Philosophy = The upper joint of the finger nearest the nail.

The Knot of Order = The lower joint of the finger nearest the palm.

The Mount of Mars. There are two, the one being found at the side of the hand between Jupiter's Mount and the thumb, the other also being found at the side of the hand, but lying immediately between the Mounts of Mercury and of Luna, opposite to the Mount of Venus.

The Mount of Luna = That portion of the hand lying between the Mount of Mars and the wrist under Mercury's finger.

The Mount of Venus = The fleshy part at the root of the thumb opposite the Mounts of Mars and Luna.

The First Angle is formed by the union of the Vital and the Cerebral at their starting point.

The Second Angle is formed by the union of Hepatica with the Vital at the root of the thumb. Should Hepatica be wanting in the hand, the Saturnian would take its place.

The Third Angle is formed by the union of Hepatica with the Cerebral.

The Triangle is formed by the Vital, Cerebral and Hepatica. Should the Hepatica be absent the Solar or Saturnian would form the Triangle in its stead. This formation is, however, unfortunate.

The Quadrangle is that portion of the hand lying between the Mensal and the Cerebral.

The Vital is the line which encircles the thumb, or Mount of Venus.

The Mensal is the line running horizontally at the base of the Mounts, otherwise called the Line of Heart.

The Cerebral or line of Head, is the line which rises between the thumb and first finger, and traverses the palm horizontally below the Mensal.

The Saturnian is the line found in the centre of the hand ascending it perpendicularly towards the Mount of Saturn. It may take its rise from the Vital, the Plain of Mars, the Mount of Luna, or the Rascette.

The Solar, or line of ⊙, is the line which slants across the palm to the finger of Apollo, rising either from the Vital, the Mensal. the Mount of Luna or the Plain of Mars.

Hepatica is the line which traverses the palm ascending towards the finger of Mercury. It generally starts either from the Vital or the Rascette.

The Plain of Mars is that portion of the hand lying between the Vital and the Cerebral.

The Girdle of Venus is a line describing a semi-circle, extending from between the Mounts of Jupiter and Saturn to the Mount of Mercury. This girdle is generally absent.

The Milky Way (Voie Lactée) is a sister line to Hepatica and is very rare.

The Line of Intuition or Line of Luna is a line

taking a circular course from the Mount of Luna towards the root of Mercury's finger.

The Line of Presentiment is formed by Hepatica curving in its course, and describing a semi-circle.

The Line of Mars is a sister line to the Vital. It is a lucky sign when found in any hand, since it promises strength, riches, and success in life, but, alas ! it is very rare.

King Solomon's Ring is a term used when the Mensal forms a circle round the Mount of Jupiter.

The Rascette or Bracelets are those lines traversing the wrist horizontally.

THE LUCKY HAND.

As my great object in writing this book is to offer the public a most·simple and complete work on the readings of the hand, the reader will, by comparing the two following diagrams, be able to see at a glance the marked difference between those who have a Lucky or Unlucky Hand. Comparisons of this kind are of great assistance in acquiring practical knowledge of the subject. It is practical knowledge that readers of this little work will acquire, and my hope is that everyone will test the worth of it for themselves.

The student will observe that stars and crosses, otherwise unfavourable signs, are auspicious as posited in this hand.

The Vital, or Line of Life, rising on the Mount of Jupiter (as here marked) denotes fame, extraordinary success, good health, and an exceptionally strong constitution, which latter is also shown by the absence of Hepatica. It is indeed most rare for the Vital to start from this Mount. The sister line to the Vital, known as the Line of Mars, gives excellent health and happiness in love. The latter is further indicated by the regular well-marked cross on Jupiter's Mount. The Mensal, or Line of Heart, is here forked both at its commencement and termination. The branches of this fork rising high on to Jupiter's Mount denote great happiness as confirmed by the Saturnian, and the straight lines on the third phalange of Apollo's finger.

The Cerebral, or Line of Head, being forked and accompanied by a sister line denotes an affluence of the goods of Fortune and a noble character. Riches are further shown by the cross lines on the joint by the side of the thumb, as also by the circle on Apollo's Mount.

The Saturnian, or Line of Fate, rising from the Rascette, and proceeding in a direct line to Saturn's Mount, there terminating in a fork, gives fame and renown either in Art or Science. Such a Rascette, or Triple Bracelet, well marked and uninterrupted promises long life, health, and prosperity.

The Solar, starting from the Vital and terminating high on Apollo's Mount, denotes honours and distinction, worldly success, and fame, here confirmed by

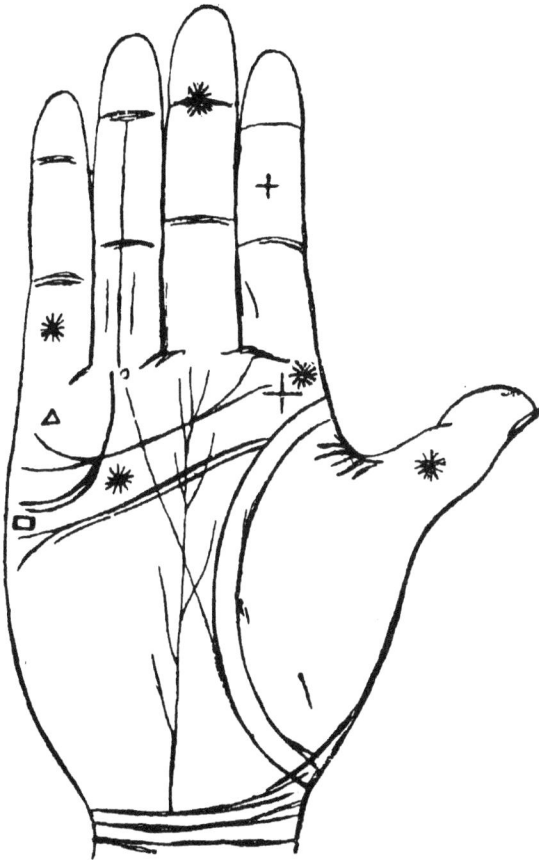

Diagram 1

The Lucky Hand.

the Line of Ambition, which cutting the Mensal
terminates high on Apollo's Mount.

The single line from the root to the first phalange
of Apollo's finger indicates great glory. The smaller
marks in this hand are also favourable, since the star
on the second phalange of the thumb denotes
amiability, on the first joint of the middle finger gives
military or political renown, on the third phalange of
Mercury's finger eloquence and skill. This is confirmed by the triangle on the Mount of Mercury, and
the star on the Mount of Jupiter near the marriage
cross riches by marriage. The crosses may also be
considered fortunate since that on Jupiter's Mount
signifies happy marriage and that on the second
phalange of Jupiter's finger the friendship of the
great. The square on the Mount of Mars indicates
courage and great presence of mind

THE UNLUCKY HAND.

THE features of this hand are as unfavourable as those of the Lucky Hand are fortunate. This short chained and forked Vital with a clearly marked cross denotes a most serious illness, a loveless life, and early death. The latter is further borne out by the short deep lines on the finger joints. The Mensal, or Line of Heart, interrupted and crossed by many small lines signify troubles and sorrow in the affections, with the probability of a broken engagement.

The Cerebral, or Line of Head, poorly marked with a circle and cross on it shows misfortune, carelessness, a poor intelligence, and failure in all undertakings.

The Saturnian, or Line of Fate, rising from below the Rascette with a circle on it, and a small island at its commencement, indicates the death of father or mother in early life, great tribulation, and a miserable fate.

Hepatica, or Line of Health, is here traversed by many small lines which, with the cross cutting it, indicate not only ill health, as confirmed by the lines on the first phalanges of the fingers, but a serious illness as well. The Vital also testifies to this.

The Line from the wrist which crosses Luna's Mount, proceeding irregularly round the percussion of the hand signifies unmitigated misfortune.

The Rascette broken and badly marked denotes great distress and poverty.

The lines from the root of the thumb, crossing the Mount of Venus and extending to the Cerebral, denote pecuniary difficulties and reverses.

The lines lying horizontally on Luna's Mount give cause for anxiety and disquietude.

The star on Luna's Mount shows danger of drowning.

The star on the Mount of Venus, with the line proceeding from it and terminating in a fork on the Mount of Saturn, shows an unfortunate marriage, which is confirmed by the cross near it signifying unhappy love.

The cross on the Vital as also that on Hepatica indicates a dangerous illness, that on the Cerebral an accident affecting the head, that on the Mount of Apollo failure in art and pecuniary difficulties. The

Diagram 2

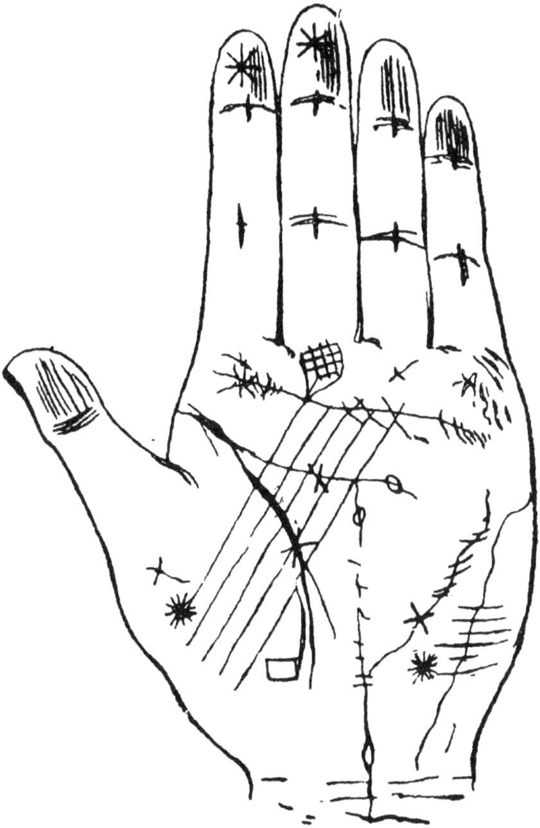

The Unlucky Hand.

waving lines on the Mount of Jupiter and Mercury point to thwarted attachments and intellectual failure.

The grill on Saturn's Mount is most ominous : dire misfortune may be expected.

The square on the Mount of Venus is also unlucky, since it corroborates the testimony of the dissevered Vital and Cerebral, namely, a loveless life. Without this confirmation this square would simply imply a secluded life.

The A B C of Palmistry.

———☙———

A.

Ability.—One or two lines on the third phalange of the finger of ☉. To bear this signification the lines must extend from the third to the second phalange.

A cross at the termination of the Vital. But though this indicates a man of ability and good character it also threatens ill-health.

Ability (Want of).—A Cerebral which only runs half way across the palm, with badly developed Mounts of ♃ and ☉. *See* Diagram 11.

Accidents (Affecting Head).—A red mark on the Cerebral, this line being broken under the Mount of ♄.

A star on the Cerebral in the middle of the Plain of Mars. *See* Diagram 10.

Accidents (from a Quadruped).—A line proceeding from the Vital direct to the Mount of ♄.

See Diagram 11. If broad at its termination and without any branches the accident will prove fatal.

A break on the Cerebral under the Mount of ☉.

Accidents (Preservation from).— A square found on any of the lines.

Accidents (Severe).—A cross in the centre of the Cerebral on the Plain of Mars.

Activity.—Hard hands with pointed fingers and the absence of Hepatica.   *See* Energy.

Acuteness. *See* Perspicacity.

Adaptability. — The Vital broken under the Mount of ☉ in the right hand only.   If seen in both hands the signification would be different.

Affectation.—Development of the Mount of ☉ to excess.

The Mount of ☉ much lined.   These lines are generally short and fagoted, and the hands are excessively smooth with tapering fingers.   *See* Diagram 9.

Affection.—The third phalange of the thumb, commonly called the Mount of ♀, well developed, but not to excess, with a good Mount of ♃. A hand with the first phalange of the thumb long and the third strongly developed denotes that the subject will allow his heart to govern his reason, especially if the Cerebral be poorly traced.

Many lines upon the Mount of ♀ unless crossed by others into a grill.

A long, clear, and well-traced Mensal. *See* Diagram 6.

The Mensal of a red colour. If this line should stretch right across the hand blind devotion is shown.

Affection (Blind).—When the Cerebral is joined to the Mensal by a line which loses itself in the Mensal a fatal infatuation is shown. *See* Diagram 4.

Affection (Disappointed).—The Mensal with a bar or bars across it.

Affection (Misplaced).—The Mount of ♄ traversed by a line which rises from the Mensal, and suddenly turns back abruptly. A small line is generally found cutting the Mensal with a deep red mark on it.

Affection (Sensuality in).—The Mensal starting from beneath the Mount of ♄ instead of under that of ♃. Diagrams 3 and 9.

The Girdle of Venus marked. *See* Diagram 3.

The Mount of ♀ unduly developed with a grill ♀n it.

The Milky Way. This is very rarely seen.

Affliction. *See* **Misfortune** and **Troubles.**

Aggressiveness. *See* Diagram 9.—The Mount of ♂ unduly developed.

The triangle raised in the palm.

The Plain of ♂ considerably raised.

Agriculture (Love of).—Spatulate fingers with the second phalange of the finger of ♄ relatively long in both hands.

Ague. *See* Diseases.

Ambition.—The Mount of ♃ high and well developed, with a good Saturnian and Solar.

A line rising from the centre of the Mount of ☽ on to the Mount of ♃.

The finger of ♃ longer in proportion than that of ♄, and the second phalange particularly so.

A branch from the Cerebral ascending the Mount of ♃ to the root of the finger. Terminating with a cross the ambition will be thwarted. A star would promise success.

Ambition (Boundless).—A line rising from the Vital on to the Mount of ♃, which ambition will be realized should the line be seen in both hands and uncrossed.

A line starting from the Mount of ♂ below the Mensal and the finger of ☿, and proceeding direct to the Mount of ☉.

This would give the determination to succeed at any cost in order to attain celebrity. *See* The Lucky Hand.   Diagram 1.

Ambition (Gratified).—The Saturnian finishing

its course on the Mount of ♃. The higher it rises the greater will be the success.

The Vital starting from the Mount of ♃. This is most exceptional, and when seen the highest honours may be expected. *See* Diagram 1. The Lucky Hand.

Ambition (Life of).—One deep line running the whole length of the finger of ♃ in both hands.

Ambition (Want or).—The Triangle much sunk in the hand and the Mount of ♃ poorly developed.

Amiability.—The Mounts of ♀ and ♃ well developed in both hands.

One or two stars on the second phalange of the thumb. *See* Diagram 8.

Amorous. *See* **Susceptibility.**

Anger. *See* **Temper.**

Animals (Love of).—The first phalanges of all the fingers short, and the finger of ♄ particularly square at the tip.

Apoplexy. *See* **Diseases.**

Application. *See* **Diligence.**

Ardour. *See* **Enthusiasm.**

Argument (**Love of**).—The second phalanges of the fingers long, especially that of ☿.

A short palm with long fingers, the nails being broader than they are long.

Art (Celebrity in).—A straight clear line from

the Cerebral to the finger of ⊙, which must be well developed.

The Saturnian running direct toward the Mount of ⊙. *See* Diagram 11.

Art (Failure in).—A cross on the Mount of ⊙. *See* Diagram 2. Smooth hands with spatulate fingers and a badly developed Mount of ⊙.

Art (Failure in, for want of Concentration). —Many tangled, forked lines on the Mount of ⊙.

Two or three lines rising from the Solar, but irregular and uneven, or crossed by others.

A branch on the Mount of ⊙, dividing itself into others so as to form the letter V.

Art (Love of).—The Mount of ⊙ well developed.

The first phalange of the finger of ⊙ very long, the finger being long and pointed, and the thumbs small. Smooth fingers without protruding joints, with lines ascending the finger of ⊙ and a long, sloping Cerebral.

Art (Originality in). — Knotted hands with pointed fingers, the first phalanges of all the fingers being much developed, and the lower joints poorly marked.

Art (Reason in).—The second phalange of the finger of ⊙ very long. *See* Diagram 5.

Art (Science in).—A triangle on the Mount of ⊙.

Art (Success in).—A line from the Vital ascending the Mount of ☉ or ☿, unless crossed out by other lines. *See* Diagram 11.

The Solar taking its rise from the Vital in both hands. *See* Diagram 1.

Asceticism. — Excessive development of the Mount of ♄, with a narrow Quadrangle. *See* **Fanaticism,** Diagram 9.

Assurance.—First phalange of the thumb long and strongly developed, with knotted hands and spatulate fingers.

Cerebral disconnected from the Vital at its starting point. In proportion as the Cerebral is long, well marked and coloured, will the subject's self-reliance be developed. *See* Diagram 7.

Audacity.—The Triangle very broad and large, with the Mount of ♂ much developed. Smooth hands with spatulate fingers, and the Mount of ☿ developed.

Avarice.—The Cerebral extending across the whole breadth of the hand in a straight line, with a badly-formed Triangle.

The finger of ☉ square, with the Cerebral better developed than the Mensal. *See* Diagram 9.

The first phalanges of all the fingers hollowed out, with a tendency to curve upwards and inwards, being joined together closely at the roots. *See* Diagram 9.

The third phalanges of the fingers of ♄ and ☉ relatively long, with the Mensal inclining towards the Cerebral. *See* Diagram 9.

The Mount of ☉ excessively developed, with thumbs that incline inwards towards the palm, all the fingers being stiff and hard.

Avarice (Boundless).—Total absence of the Mensal.

A line proceeding from the Mensal direct to the finger of ☿, this mount being well developed. *See* Diagram 9.

B.

Bankruptcy.—An island on Hepatica and the Saturnian cut up by small lines, the Solar being absent or badly traced.

Benevolence.—The Saturnian taking its rise from the Vital with the Mounts of ♃ and ♀ well developed. *See* Diagram 5.

The Triangle broad and well traced. A wide quadrangle clearly defined. *See* Diagram 8.

Biliousness.—A cold damp hand with Hepatica undulating and tortuous.

Blindness.—A star on the Plain of Mars near the Hepatica

Diagram 3

A Profligate Hand.

Two small circles on the Mount of ☽ or on the Vital.

A cross high up on Hepatica with a circle on the Cerebral.

Brain-Disease.—A tortuous Cerebral inclining towards Hepatica, with the Saturnian terminating abruptly at the Cerebral.

Hepatica united to the Cerebral with the Vital intersected by many fine lines.

A pale and wide Cerebral dotted with black flecks, and the Vital bifurcated.

Brain-Fever.—The Vital deviating from its usual course, and slanting towards the Cerebral.

The Vital cut by a line which, starting from the Mount of   , crosses the Plain of Mars and terminates in a point or star on the Cerebral.

Bravado.—The Mount of ☉ developed to excess with a grill, and the finger of ☉ pointed in both hands, the other fingers being spatulate or square-tipped.

Bravery.—The Triangle raised in both hands.

The Mount of ♂ well developed but not lined, with the Plain of ♂ raised.

Fingers very straight, particularly in the third phalanges. *See* Diagram 8.

Bravery (Indomitable).—The Mount of ♂ under Jupiter well developed, with spatulate fingers shorter than the palm, and somewhat hirsute on the phalanges.

Bravery (Passive).—The Mount of ♂ under Mercury well developed, the fingers being square and the hands firm to the touch.

Broadmindedness.—A wide Quadrangle with a good Cerebral, and the second phalange of the thumb well developed.   *See* Diagram 8.

Brusqueness.—The Vital hollowed out in both hands and deeply traced, presenting a red colour, and completely disconnected from the Cerebral at its commencement.

The Mount of ♂ unduly developed, with a poor Mount of ♀, and that of ☿ flat. Such subjects have generally knotted hands with spatulate fingers.

Business (Aptitude for).—The Mount of ☿ so much developed as to encroach on the Mount of ☉.

Square finger tips with large curved nails, the first phalange of the finger of ☿ being long and square.

Business (Failure in).—The Saturnian rising from below the Rascette and terminating at the Cerebral, this line being short.   *See* Diagram 2.

A narrow Triangle caused by the Vital inclining toward the Cerebral.

Business (Success in).—A line from the wrist crossing the Cerebral and proceeding to the Mount of ☿.

The Cerebral throwing branches on to a well-formed Mount of ☿.

The Saturnian terminating its course on the Mount of ☿. *See* Diagram 3.

C.

Calamity.—A line starting from the Cerebral and terminating by a cross on the Mount of ♃ in an otherwise unlucky hand. *See* **Troubles, Unhappiness.**

Capital Punishment.—The Cerebral broken beneath the Mount of ♄ with a cross in the Plain of Mars, and the Vital terminating abruptly. *See* **Death.**

Captiousness.—The Mount of ☽ unduly developed with a circle on the Plain of Mars.

The Line of Intuition short, tortuous and branched, with the Mounts of   well developed.

Two stars near the thumb nails.

The Hepatica traversing the Mount of ☽ and running close to the percussion of the hand, with the Mounts of ☿ and ☽ much developed. Diagram 9.

Carelessness.—The finger of ♄ pointed. Diagram 9. *See* **Imprudence.**

Casualties.—Change in business is shown by Hepatica throwing branches towards the Solar.

Crosses near Hepatica but not on it. A cross on the Saturnian. If near but not on the line the change will affect the life of a near relation or intimate friend.

A break in the Saturnian. Under favourable circumstances, and if the Saturnian continues its course, the change would be for the better, but with a poor Saturnian traversed by small lines misfortune is to be apprehended. *See* Diagram 2.

A cross in the Triangle.

A cross low down in the base of the hand lying between the Mounts of ♀ and ☽. The change in this case would be the outcome of some conflict.

Casualties (Favourable).—A star on the first phalange of the finger of ♃.

Casualties (Unfavourable).—A star on the first phalange of the finger of ♄. *See* Diagram 2.

Caution.—The first phalange of the thumb curving inwards when the other fingers are upright.

Celebrity (Attained by Chance).—A good Saturnian with a star on the Mount of ☉

Parallel lines on the Mount of ☉ if well marked and uncrossed in both hands.

Celebrity (Attained By Talent).—One single line well traced with a star on the Mount of ☉ and the Solar clearly defined in both hands.

Celibacy.—A cross on the first phalange of the finger of ☿. *See* Diagram 11.

Censoriousness.—The Mount of ☽ very low, with the Mount of ♄ well developed.

Character (Clergyman).—The upper and lower knots of the fingers are usually well developed, with pointed finger tips.

Character (Inferiority of).—The Mensal descending towards the Cerebral, thus forming a narrow Quadrangle. *See* Diagram 9.

Character (Nobility of).—One or two straight lines running from the third to the second phalange of the finger of ☉ with a wide Quadrangle, and the Triangle well formed. *See* Diagram 8.

Charity.—The Mounts of ♀ and ♃ well developed, and a well-formed Mensal.

Chastity.—A cross on the first phalange of the finger of ☉ with a good Mount of ♃. *See* Diagram 8.

Cheerfulness.—The first phalange of Mercury's finger long, with the Mounts of ☿ and ♃ both well developed.

Hard hands, with the Mount of ♀ pronounced and that of ♄ low.

Chemistry (Love of).—Short upright lines near the percussion of the hand on the Mount of ☿.

Childhood (Unhappy).—Saturnian commencing with zigzags or a series of crosses. *See* Diagram 8.

Children.—Short lines from the root of the finger of ☿ moving down toward the marriage line on the percussion of the hand.

Clairvoyance.—The line of intuition or line of Luna commencing with an island.

The Cerebral terminating in a long fine fork on the Mount of ☽. *See* Diagram 9.

King Solomon's Ring, which is formed by the Mensal circling round the finger of ♃.

Hepatica forming a kind of semicircle from the Mount of ☽ to that of ☿. *See* Diagram 10.

Cleverness. *See* **Understanding.**

Coldness.—The absence of the Mensal. *See* **Dispassionate.**

Combativeness. *See* **Temper.**—Very short, broad finger nails with the Mount of ♂ much developed.

Comfort (Love of).—The palm of the same length as the fingers, and these rather square tipped with the third phalanges particularly developed.

Commerce (Aptitude for).—The finger of ☉ square in both hands. *See* Diagram 9.

The second phalange of the finger of ☿ relatively long and well developed.

Common Sense.—The first and second phalanges

of the thumb of equal length, and the thumbs longer in proportion than the fingers.

The Cerebral long, straight and clear. *See* Diagram 8.

The second phalange of the finger of ☿ very long. *See* Diagram 1.

Complaints (Headache).—Hepatica of a red colour near the Cerebral.

Complaints (Hereditary).—An island on the Vital. *See* **Disease.**

Complaints (Hysteria).—The Mounts of ♀ and ☽ strongly developed, with the Girdle of Venus intersected by many lines.

Complaints (Indigestion).—An island on Hepatica.

Complaints (Internal).—The Vital and Hepatica of a yellow colour.

Complaints (Liver).—The Cerebral irregular in its course, either winding or discoloured, with a dark bluish spot on it.

Complaints (Nervous).—Small dark clots on the Vital with a cold dry skin.

Conceit.—The Mounts of ♃ and ☉ unduly large

A spatulate hand with the Cerebral and Vital far apart at their commencement.

Concentration.—A well-developed Cerebral, with good Mounts of ♃ and ☿.

Concentration (Want of). — Two or more unequal, irregular lines on the Mount of ⊙, with that of ☿ abnormally large.

A short chained Cerebral, or long, fine, and very faintly traced.

Conscientiousness.—A spatulate hand with the thumb well developed, and the Mount of ♃ good.

Constancy.—Many lines ascending the thumb, but they must not be crossed into a grill. *See* Diagram 7.

The Mount of ♀ moderately developed, with the Cerebral long and narrow. *See* Diagram 7.

One cross on the Mount of ♀, with large thumbs, the first and third phalanges being long.

A well-traced Mensal, forked under the Mount of ♃, and running a considerable distance. *See* Diagram 6.

Consumption.—Wide fluted nails, curved at the top, and the Cerebral formed of little islands.

Contempt (For opposite Sex).—The Mensal taking its rise under the finger of ♄ and formed of chains. *See* **Superciliousness.**

Conventionality.—The hand having a natural tendency to curl up towards the palm when held loosely open, and the Quadrangle narrow.

The Mensal inclining towards the Cerebral, and

the latter connected with the Vital for some distance. *See* Diagram 4.

Coquetry.—The Mount of ♀ developed to excess, with a chained Mensal poorly traced.

Covetousness.   *See* Avarice.

Cowardice.   *See* Pusillanimity.

Craft.—The finger of ☿ crooked.

The Cerebral sloping and ending in a fork on the Mount of ☽. *See* Diagram 9.

Credulity.—Pointed fingers with the knot of philosophy. *See* **Superstition.**

Criticism.—Well-formed short nails with long fingers.

Cruelty.—Entire absence of the Mensal, with a large intervening space between the Cerebral and the Vital, both lines being of a red colour.

The Quadrangle narrow and formed by red lines, with a short Mensal and the Mount of ♂ largely developed. *See* Diagram 9.

Red-coloured nails flecked with white.

Curiosity.—The Mount of ☉ unduly developed and all the fingers supple, inclining backwards and outwards.

D.

Danger (from Animals).—A star on the Mount of ♄ or ♂. *See* Diagram 10.

A horizontal bar in the exact centre of the Mount of ☽, running towards the percussion.

Danger (of Assassination).—A star on the third phalange of the finger of ♄.

A line rising below the Mount of ♄ and ascending to cut the Ring of Venus.

Danger (of Shipwreck or Drowning).—A star or acute angle on the Mount of ☽, situated on a voyage line. *See* Diagram 2.

Lines rising from the Bracelet and terminating on the Mount of ☽ with a star.

Danger (Threatened).—A star or stars on the Saturnian is a forewarner of some imminent danger

A cross on the Vital in both hands. *See* Diagram 2.

Daring Spirit.—The Mensal extending round the percussion of the hand with a long and clear Cerebral and the Mounts of ♂ well developed. *See* Diagram 8.

Death (in Battle).—A star on the Mount of ♂

An oblique line rising from the Mount of ♂ to the Mount of ♄.

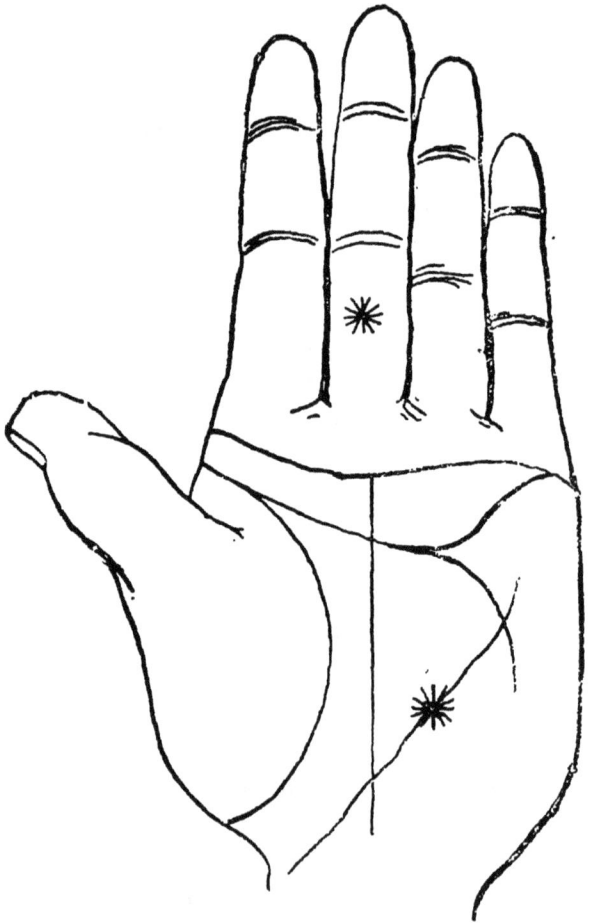

Diagram 4

Blind Affection Causing Sorrow

Death (Dishonourable).—Two stars on the third phalange of the finger of ☿.

The Saturnian of a deep red colour, cutting through the finger of ♄, and rising above the third phalange. *See* Diagram 10.

Death (by Drowning).—The Cerebral descending and losing itself on the Mount of ☽, with a star on this mount.

Death (on the Scaffold).—Two stars, one on the Mount of ♄, the other on the third phalange of the same finger.

The Cerebral broken into small sections under the finger of ♄, the broken lines overlying each other; but this must be seen in both hands and be further confirmed by other unfavourable signs.

Death (Premature).—A cross on the centre of the Cerebral, with the Mensal or Cerebral stopping abruptly at the Saturnian.

The Vital broken in both hands, or very short and ending suddenly. *See* Diagram 10.

The Cerebral rising to join the Mensal under the finger of ☿ in a tortuous circle.

Death (Sudden).—One short line deeply traced on the joints of all the fingers. *See* Diagram 10.

The Cerebral, Mensal, and Vital uniting together under the finger of ♃, with a cross in the centre of the Cerebral.

Death (Violent).—A cross on the Saturnian at its termination, with a grill on the Mount of ♂.

The Cerebral sloping to the Rascette and terminating in a cross or star.

Debility.—Many small lines resembling creases on the first phalange of each finger, the nails of which are narrow. *See* **Health.**

Deceit.—The Quadrangle narrow in its centre, and the third phalange of the finger of ☿ relatively long. *See* Diagrams 9 and 10.

The Cerebral terminating in a large irregular fork, and sloping towards the Mount of ☽. *See* Diagram 9.

The third phalanges of all the fingers shaped like a waist.

The Mount of ☿ unduly developed, and the fourth finger crooked or tapering.

Cross bars on the Mount of ☿. *See* Diagram 9.

Deference to Opinion.—Excessively square finger tips with the Cerebral and Vital connected.

Deliberation.—The second phalange of the thumb well developed and a total absence of lines on the finger of ♄.

Delirium Tremens.—A line rising from the Vital and terminating in a star on the Mount of ☽, with a black fleck on the Cerebral in both hands. *See* **Intemperance.**

Dependence.—The first phalange of the thumb very short and narrow in both hands with the Cerebral and Vital connected at the commencement of their course. *See* Diagram 4.

Depravity.—A triangle on the Mount of ♄, accompanied by a star on the first phalange of this finger. *See* **Profligacy.** Diagram 9.

Despondency. — The Mount of ♄ largely developed, and the Saturnian terminating at the Cerebral or Mensal. *See* Diagram 4.

Despotism. — The Mount of ♂ excessively developed and much lined, with the first phalange of the thumbs strong. *See* **Tyranny.**

Destiny (A Grand).—The Saturnian rising from the Rascette and entering the finger of ♄ to the third phalange denotes a most extraordinary fate, whether for good or ill must be judged by the general bearing of the hand.

Detail (Incapacity for).—Smooth conical shaped fingers.

Detail (Love of).—A long Cerebral with hands and fingers also long.

Determination.—Many lines from the Mount of ♃ crossing the Mount to the third phalange. A fork on the Mount of ☉ with strong thumbs. *See* **Will Power.**

Devotion.—The Mount of ♂ under the finger of

☿ full, with a good Mensal and the Mount of ♀ well developed.

Dexterity. *See* **Skill.**

Difficulties.—A line branching from the wrist and advancing to the Mount of ♂. *See* **Troubles.** Diagram 2.

Diffidence.—The Cerebral closely connected with the Vital at its commencement. Diagram 5.

Diligence.—The second phalange of the finger of ☿ relatively long, with the Mounts of ♃ and ♂ well developed.

Diplomacy.—A pointed finger of ☿ with a triangle on the Mount.

Disappointment (Caused by Loved Ones).— Downward branches from the Mensal.

Disappointments (Throughout Life). — The Vital throwing off small branches towards the Rascette. *See* **Unhappiness.**

Discernment. *See* **Judgment and Reason.**

Discontent.—The Mount of ☽ excessively large, with long fingers square tipped.

Cross bars on the Mount of ☽.

A circle enclosing the finger of ☿.

Discoveries.—White spots on the Cerebral. *See* **Invention.**

Diseases (Ague).—A black fleck on the first

phalange of the finger of ♄, so situated as to be concealed when the hand is closed.

Diseases (Apoplexy). — Hepatica of varying colour, and red where it crosses the Cerebral. Death from apoplexy is indicated by two perpendicular lines proceeding straight from the Mensal to the Mount of ☽.

Diseases (Asthma).—The Quadrangle narrow, with an imperfectly-traced Hepatica, and the Mensal sinking toward the Cerebral.

Disease (Brain).—The Vital intersected by lines rising from the Cerebral, with the Mount of ☿ well developed.

Disease (Consumption).—Fluted nails curved at their tips. *See* **Complaints** and **Pleurisy.**

Disease (Dropsy).—A star on the Mount of ☽, but not on a voyage line, as this would give another signification.

Diseases (Gout).—The Vital biforked at its termination, with one branch proceeding towards the Mount of ☽ .

Diseases (Heart).—The Mensal very pale and wide, particularly beneath the finger of ♄.

An island on the Solar accompanied by signs of illness on the Vital.

The Hepatica closely connected with the Vital and irregular in its course, with red or bluish flecks on the Vital.

Disease (Hereditary).—Islands on the Vital.

Disease (Liver).—The Cerebral tortuous, irregular, and of changing colour.

Disease (Paralysis).—A star at the termination of the Vital in both hands. Death will ensue if there is also a star at the Saturnian's termination.

Disease (Pleurisy).—A line rising from the Vital and ending in an island on the Mount of ♃.

Dishonesty.—A grill or cross on the finger of ☿. *See* **Theft**, Diagram 9.

Dishonour.—A star on the Mount of ☿ with the Mount of ♃ low.

Disorder.—Smooth hands, with tapering fingers and the knots undeveloped.

Dispassion.—The Mount ot ♀ flat and smooth, or covered by many lines crossed by others into a grill.

The Cerebral both wide and pale, with a poor Mensal.

The hands square, with the knots developed.

The Mensal inclining towards the Cerebral.

Dissipation.—The Mensal pale and broad. *See* **Profligacy.**

Divorce.—A line running from the Mount of ♀ to the Mensal, there terminating in a fork, and confirmed by an island on the Saturnian.

The marriage line terminating in a fork and drooping towards the Mensal. *See* Diagram 8.

Dogmatism.—Excessively smooth hands, with long stiff fingers, square at their tips. *See* **Tyranny.**

Domineering.—The third phalange of the finger of ♃ longer than the others in both hands, with the first phalange of the thumbs strong.

Drowning (Danger of).—An angle on the Mount of ☽.

Transverse waving lines on the first phalange of all the fingers. *See* **Death.**

Dulness.—The Cerebral pale and broad, with hard hands and the Mount of ☉ low. *See* **Understanding (Want of).**

Duplicity.—The Mensal approaching the Cerebral so as to form a very narrow Quadrangle, with the Mount of ☽ raised. *See* **Deceit, Hypocrisy,** and Diagram 9.

E.

Ebriety.—A line rising from the Vital, and terminating in a star on the Mount of ☽, with other unfavourable indications.

A branch from the line of ♂ sloping on to the Mount of ☽.

Economy.—The Cerebral very long and straight, with a good Mensal, and the first finger relatively longer than the rest.

Effrontery.—The Mounts of ♀ and ☿ unduly large.

Egotism.—The Mount of ♃ excessively developed, with a grill.

The Quadrangle narrow, and the Triangle badly formed, with the Mount of ☉ raised. *See* Diagram 9.

The Mount of ♀ low and poor, with the Mensal short and faintly traced.

The lower phalanges and knots of fingers much developed, and the absence of the Mensal.

Egotism (Combined with Self-Esteem).—The Mounts of ☽ and ♀ flat in both hands, with the others raised, especially that of ♃.

The Mounts of ♃ and ♀ very low, with the Cerebral running to the percussion of the hand and the thumb inclining inward, with the fingers close together.

Egotism (Intense).—A poor Mount of ♀, with a grill on it. *See* Diagram 9.

A Cerebral which, after traversing the palm, circles round in the direction of the thumb.

A thick, smooth, white skin, which remains unaffected by temperature, with soft, flabby hands and raised mounts, the fingers being spatulate in both hands.

A short Mensal without any branches rising or

falling from it, and stopping beneath the Mount of ♄. *See* Diagram 3.

Eloquence.—The finger of ☿ pointed and relatively long, especially in the first phalange.

The Mount of ☿ well developed, with a star on the third phalange of this finger.

The Cerebral long and sloping toward the Mount of ☽, and the Mount of ♃ strongly developed with a grill.

A small triangle posted at the lower extremity of the Cerebral.

Eloquence (Great). — The Saturnian sloping toward the Mount of ☉. *See* Diagram 11.

Endurance.—The Mount of ♂ under the fourth finger largely developed.

Enemies.—Transverse lines on the Mount of ♂ crossing the percussion of the hand.

Energy.—The Cerebral long and narrow with the Mounts of ♂, ♃ and ☿ developed.

The Saturnian rising from the Plain of Mars.

The Mount of ♂ encroaching on the Mount of ☿.

A hard firm hand deeply lined with knotted spatulate fingers, and the Vital and Cerebral disconnected at their start.

Energy (Mental).—Soft smooth hands with spatulate fingers, the finger of ♄ being particularly so, and lines ascending the first finger.

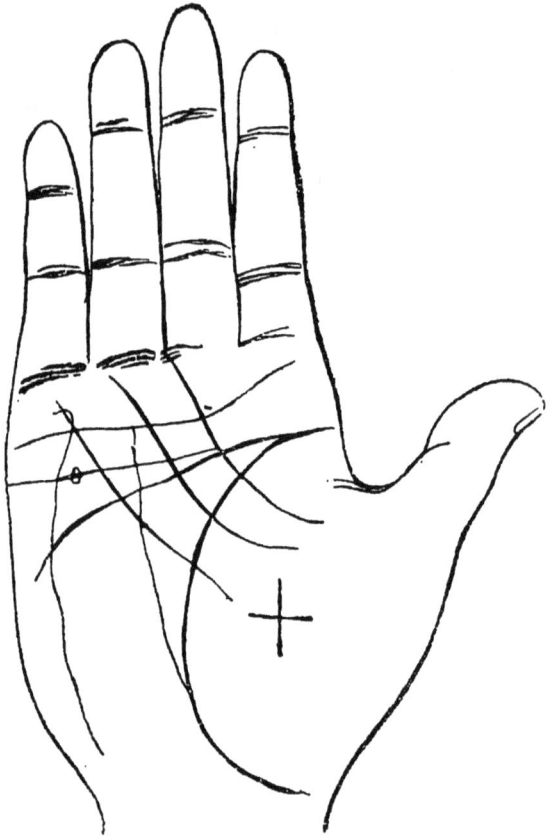

Diagram 5

Life Wrecked by Love.

Engagements (Broken).—A break in the Mensal
If this occurs under the Mount of ♄ it will be the
result of unforeseen circumstances not under the
subject's control. If under ☉ it would signify that
money parted the lovers, and if under ☿ the break
would signify caprice.

The marriage line on the Mount of ☿ forked on
one side. If forked on the inside of the hand the
engagement will have been broken off by the subject
in whose hand the fork is seen.

Enterprise (Love of).—The finger of ☉ very
long in both hands.

Enthusiasm.—Long tapering fingers and smooth
joints. The palm of the hand narrow with a short
thumb.

Enthusiasm (Exaggerated).—A badly-formed
cross in the Quadrangle, with the Vital and Cerebral
disconnected at their starting point.

Enthusiasm (Want of).—Hands with excessively
square finger tips.

Envy.—Many transverse lines on the second and
third phalange of the finger of ♃.

The Mount of ♃ and ☉ much developed with
horizontal lines barring it.

An undue development of the Mount of ☉ with
a curved circle surrounding the finger.

Events.—An enterprise of some kind is marked

by a straight line from the Vital to the Mount of ♄.
See Diagram 11.

Wrinkled lines cutting the Vital denote as many
events or changes to happen as there are lines.
Whether these events will be favourable or the
reverse depends on the Saturnian.

Events (Causing an Entire Change in Life).
—The Vital biforked at its termination, or a cross
low down in the hand near the wrist.

Events (Fatal).—The Mensal joining the Cerebral
under the finger of ♄.

A star on the first phalange of the finger of ♄
See Diagram 2.

Events (Fortunate but Late in Life).—A
cross on the lower part of the Triangle.

Exaggeration in Thought and Action.—The
finger of ♃ spatulate.

Excessively smooth hands with tapering fingers.

Extravagance.--The first phalange of all the
fingers inclining naturally outwards, the thumb most
particularly.

Eyesight (Loss of).—A small circle on the Vital
or Cerebral. *See* Blindness and Diagram 2.

F.

Failure.—The Vital terminating in a series of crosses in both hands with a poor Saturnian.

The Mount of ☉ cut up by numerous hairlines.

The Solar terminating in a series of small lines when near the Mount of ☉.

Fainting Fits.—A tendency to such is shown when the Cerebral approaches the Mensal and Hepatica rises from the Vital.

Faithfulness. *See* **Constancy.**

Faithlessness.—The Mounts of ♀ and ☿ strongly developed. *See* Diagram 9.

The Mensal weak and poorly traced with a chained Cerebral. *See* Diagram 9.

The third Angle very obtuse, with the first phalange of the thumb weak and the third strong.

Falsehood.—The Mount of ☽ strongly developed with long fingers and a short thumb. Many confused marks on the finger of ☿.

A cross on the Mount of ☽ but not on a voyage line, with the Cerebral terminating in a fork. *See* Diagram 9.

Fame.—The Solar clearly marked in both hands and not crossed by other lines.

A star on the Mount of ♃. *See* **Celebrity.**

Fame (Signal).—A line rising from the root of the finger of ☉ and terminating at the joint of the first phalange.

Family (Absence of any).—A star on Hepatica. *See* Diagram 4.

A star on the third phalange of the finger of ♄. *See* Diagram 4. A poor thin Mensal near the percussion of the hand.

Family (Affection).—The fingers and palm of the same length, with the Mount of ♃ developed.

Fanaticism.—A branch from the Cerebral rising high on to the Mount of ♃, and then proceeding to the Mount of ♄.

The Mount of ♃ unduly developed, with excessively smooth hands, and tapering fingers.

Fatality.—The Vital rising from the Mount of ☽. This is very rare.

The Saturnian rising from the Rascette and entering the finger of ♄ . *See* Diagram 10.

Many lines crossing the Mount of ♀ to the palm, with a star on the Mount of ♃.

The Mensal joined by the Cerebral under the finger of ♄.

The Mount of ♄ much developed with a cross on it.

Faultfinding (Love of).—A long hand with the

knots of philosophy much developed and spatulate fingers.

Fever.—Both Hepatica and the Vital very narrow and highly coloured, with dark flecks on the Cerebral.

Fever (Brain).—An island on the Cerebral with Hepatica red as it nears the Cerebral.

Financial Failure.—A cross on the Mount of ☿, so close to the Mensal as to cause one of its branches to cut this line.

Financial Success.—White flecks on the Cerebral under the Mount of ♄.

Firmness.—The first phalange of the thumb long and broad, with the Mounts of ♃ and ☉ pronounced.

Flirtations.—A chained Mensal. If very serious these may take the form of islands.

Folly.—The Cerebral rising toward the Mensal in a tortuous curve under the finger of ☉ or ☿.

Foresight.—A large thumb with the first and second phalange equally developed. The palm of a medium size, hollow and firm, with square phalanges to all the fingers. *See* **Prudence.**

Forgiving Disposition.—Filbert nails.

Fortitude. *See* **Endurance.**

Fortune (Brilliant).—The Solar rising from the Vital.

A line from the Cerebral terminating in a star on the Mount of ♃.

The Saturnian starting from the Rascette and rising to the first joint of the middle finger in a clear and straight line.

Fortune (Following a Laborious Life).—The Rascette chained, but even and uninterrupted.

Fortune (Good).—The Cerebral and Mensal forked under the Mount of ♃. *See* Diagram 1.

A single deep line on the Mount of ☿.

One deep clear line on the Mount of ♃.

A line extending from the Mount of ♀ to that of ☿ gives both love and fortune.

Fortune (Late in Life).—The Vital rising from the Plain of Mars with a good Saturnian.

Fortune (Owing to Another's Caprice).—The Saturnian starting from the Mount of ☽ and continuing uninterrupted and clearly defined to the Mount of ♄. *See* Diagram 6.

Friendship of the Great.—One or two crosses on the second phalange of the first finger. *See* Diagram 1.

A well-traced line starting from the Quadrangle to the Mount of ☿.

The Solar deeply traced and well marked with the Mount of ♃ large in both hands. *See* **Glory** and **Honours.**

Frivolity.—The finger of ♄ pointed. *See* Diagram 9. This is rare.

The Mount of ☉ unduly large, with a grill.

The finger of ☉ pointed, with all the others either spatulate or square.

The Cerebral narrow and feeble.

G.

Gaiety.—The Mounts of ♃, ♀ and ☿ large. *See* **Cheerfulness.**

Gain in Commerce. — One clear well-traced line rising from the Cerebral toward the Mount of ☿. If it should run up between the third and little finger success in art would follow. *See* **Success.**

Gambling.—A long, narrow sloping Cerebral, with the second and third fingers nearly of the same length, and the Solar in both hands.

Generosity.—The Mensal long, straight and narrow, terminating in a fork, with the Triangle large and well traced. *See* Diagram 8.

The thumb turning outwards, the fingers also inclining backward.

Genius.—The Mount of ☉ much developed. Should this be also the case with the Mount of ☿ the genius will show itself in invention.

The thumb set very low in both hands, with the Mount of ☿ so large as to extend to the percussion of the hand.

Genius (Dramatic).—The finger of ☉ spatulate, with the Mount developed. *See* Diagram 10.

Genius (Misdirected).—Two waving irregular lines on the Mount of ☉, and a good Solar.

Genius (Rewarded).—One single deep clearly traced line on the Mount of ☉ with the Solar well defined in both hands.

Gentleness.—The Mounts of ☉ and ♀ well developed, with that of ♂ flat in the hand.

One or two stars on the second phalange of the thumb. *See* **Amiability,** and Diagram 8.

Giddiness.—A Cerebral, which rises toward the Mensal at its termination. *See* **Frivolity.**

Glory.—The Solar terminating in three even branches of the same length, one inclining toward the Mount of ☉, and another toward that of ♄. *See* **Honours.**

Goodness. —The first phalanges of all the fingers well developed, with the Mounts of ♃, ☉, and ♀ raised.

Grace.—The Mounts of ☉, ♀ and ☽ raised.

Greed.—The Cerebral traversing the palm in a horizontal line extending to the percussion, with the fingers inclining inward toward the palm.

The Mounts of ☿ and ☉ raised, with that of ☽ very flat, and the third phalanges of all the fingers long and thick.

Grief.—The Saturnian and Vital intersected by many lines cutting them horizontally.

Grief (Caused by Opposite Sex). — The Saturnian throwing an offshoot on to the Mount of ☽.

Three stars inside the Line of Mars on the Mount of ♀.

Grief (Intense).—The Saturnian taking its rise from below the Rascette. *See* Diagram 2.

A line starting from the Rascette and traversing the Mount of ☽ across the Mount of ♂ to the percussion of the hand. *See* **Disappointment** and **Unhappiness,** Diagram 2.

H.

Happiness.—One straight line on the third phalange of the finger of ☉. *See* Diagram 6.

A single clear line on the Mount of ♄, with rays tending upward from it.

One single, deep, unbroken line forming the Rascette.

Happiness (Domestic).—A straight, regular well-marked Saturnian rising from the Rascette, if uncrossed, bears this signification; but the Saturnian must terminate high on the Mount of ♄ or ♃. *See* Diagram 1.

Happiness from Merit.—The Saturnian rising from the Vital and proceeding uncrossed to the Mount of ♄.

Happiness in Love.—A clear well-marked line starting from the Mount of ♀ and running direct to that of ☿. The line must not be tortuous or crossed. Diagram 6.

The Mensal well traced, and terminating in a fork, one branch of which ascends the Mount of ♃. *See* Diagram 1.

Happiness (Intense).—The Vital accompanied by a sister line called the Line of Mars. *See* Diagram 1.

Hepatica followed by a sister line — the Milky Way.

Happiness (Negative).—The Mount of ♃ well developed, without lines across it, the Mensal terminating in a fork, one branch of which runs up between the first and second finger, with the absence of any lines or marks on the Mount of ☽.

The Mensal rising from between the fingers of ♃ and ♄.

Happiness (Unexpected).—The Saturnian rising

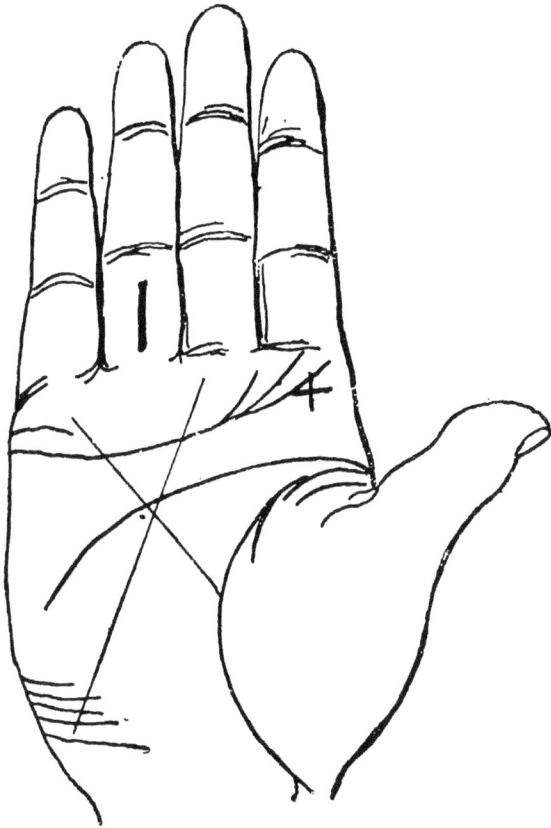

Diagram 6

Domestic Happiness.

from the Mount of ☽ direct and clear to the Mensal, and there losing itself, the Mensal then proceeding to the Mount of ♃.

Headaches.—The Cerebral formed like links or chains.

Small lines cutting the Cerebral or falling from it.

The third Angle badly formed and small lines cutting the Vital. *See* **Neuralgia.**

Health (Good).—The triple Bracelet clearly traced. The entire absence of Hepatica. *See* Diagram 1.

A narrow, long, well-coloured Vital completely encircling the Mount of ♀. *See* Diagram 1.

The Second Angle well formed and the Triangle broad.

Health (Perfect).—The line of Mars in both hands. Hepatica followed by a sister line.

Health (Poor).—A long, pale, badly-formed Vital cut by numerous small lines.

A cross at the termination of the Vital. Cerebral and Hepatica imperfect.

Many lines on the first phalange of all the fingers. *See* Diagram 2.

Heart (Weak).—Hepatica rising from the Vital and badly formed with large nails of a bluish colour.

A total absence of the Mensal and a poor Cerebral, with a tortuous Hepatica. *See* **Diseases.**

Heartlessness. The Mounts of ☉ and ♀ flat

in both hands with a straight, poorly-developed Mensal devoid of branches.

Homicide.—A cross or grill on the Mount of ♂ when accompanied by a narrow Quadrangle with a long broad and straight Mensal poorly traced and the Mount of ♂ strongly developed.

Honesty (Doubtful).—A tortuous undulating Cerebral with a narrow Quadrangle and the Mount of ☿ much raised.   *See* Diagram 9.

Honour (Keen Sense of).—One deep line running the entire length of all the fingers.

Honours and Distinction.—Many branches on the Rascette.

A line from the Rascette traversing the Plain of Mars to the Mount of ☉.

Honours Conferred by Friendships of the Great.—A line from the root of the finger of ☿ sloping down the Mount.

Honours (Episcopal).—A line from the Rascette cutting the Cerebral and Mensal and ascending the Mount of ♄ or ♃.

Honours (Great).—A star in the Quadrangle. *See* Diagram 1.

A single line passing from the root of the third finger to the first phalange.   *See* Diagram 1.

Honours (Military).—A triangle or star on the Mount of ♂.

Honours (Riches).—Branches ascending from the Vital toward the centre of the Cerebral.

Should these lines terminate on the Plain of Mars honour would only be acquired after great difficulty.

Honours (as a Statesman).—A star on the first joint of the finger of ♃ or on the Mount. *See* Diagram 1.

Hydrophobia (Danger of).—A star on the Mount of ☽ in both hands.

Hypocrisy.—The Mounts of ☿ and ☽ prominent with a cross or grill on them. *See* Diagram 9.

The third phalange of the finger of ☿ very long and thick. The Cerebral long sloping and forked at its termination, one branch descending toward the Mount of ☽ and the other ascending to the Mount of ☿.

Hysteria.—The Mounts of ♀ and ☽ highly developed with the Ring of Venus cut up by numerous small lines.

I.

Idealism.—The Bracelets curving upwards toward the palm with the Cerebral sloping toward the Mount of ☾.

A small palm, with smooth fingers, the third phalanges poorly developed and the first tapering.   The
thumbs would be small in such a hand.

Idealism in Affection.—The Mensal throwing
branches on to the Mount of ♃, and forked at its
commencement.   *See* Diagram 6.

Idiocy.—A poor Cerebral and abnormally small
thumbs.

A line from the Cerebral running direct to the
Mount of ♃ and cutting the root of this finger, with
the Saturnian following the same direction threatens
idiocy.

Ill-Health at the Close of Life.—The Vital
terminating in a series of crosses, with a broad
Hepatica interrupted at its termination.

Ill-Nature. *See* **Malevolence.**

Illness.—The Vital either crossed by small lines or
with an island on it.

A cross on the Hepatica.   *See* Diagram 2.

Hepatica intersected by small lines and the Vital
irregularly coloured.

Illness (Dangerous).—A break or fleck on
Hepatica or the Vital, with the Vital poor in one
hand and broken in the other.   Diagram 7.

A cross on the Vital in both hands or on the
Hepatica.   *See* Diagram 2.

Illness (from Sorrow in the Affections).—A

line from the Mount of ♀ crossing over to the Mensal with accompanying signs of illness.

The Vital intersected by lines from the Mensal, and a line from the Vital proceeding to the Mensal.

Illness (Serious).—The Vital broken, and one branch turning inwards toward the thumb.

The Mensal broken under the Mount of ♄ with the two pieces overlying each other. *See* Diagram 11.

Imagination.—The Mount of ☽, much developed, with fingers longer than the palm and tapering.

The Cerebral long and sloping toward ☽, especially if connected with the Vital at its commencement. *See* Diagrams 3 and 6.

Imagination (Erroneous).—The Cerebral terminating in a large fork near the Mount of ☽, or sloping almost to the Rascette. *See* Diagram 9.

Imagination (Fatal).—A star on the Mount of ☽, with a sloping or poor Cerebral.

A line rising from the Mount of ☽ and cutting the Saturnian without crossing the Cerebral.

Imagination (Over vivid).—Cross bars on the Mount of ☽ and the Mount of ♂ encroaching on the Mount of ☽.

Hepatica forming a cross with the Cerebral on the Mount of ☽.

Immorality.—A star on the first phalange of the thumb with the Mount of ♀ excessively developed. *See* Diagram 3.

A star on the third phalange of the finger of ♃, or on the second phalange if enclosed by a half circle. *See* **Profligacy**; Diagram 3.

Impatience.—The Plain of Mars much lined with the Mounts of ☿ and ♂ raised.

Impressionability.—A soft hand much lined with tapering fingers and short thumbs.

Imprisonment.—A square on the Mount of ♀ or ♂ when seen in a bad hand. *See* Diagram 2.

Imprudence.—The Vital and Cerebral running far apart at their commencement with the Mount of ♄ very flat in both hands and that of ♂ raised.

Very smooth hands with spatulate fingers.

The finger of ♄ pointed and the mount flat. *See* Diagram 9.

Impulsiveness.—Short hands, the palms being longer than the fingers, the latter supple and lined with a very pointed full thumb inclining backwards.

The finger of ♄ much lined.

Inconstancy.—A crescent on the Triangle. *See* **Unfaithfulness.**

Indecision. *See* **Vacillation.**

Independence.—The upper joints of the fingers, viz., the Knot of Philosophy much developed, large thick hands with conical finger tips and long thumbs.

Independence (of Action).—Hands in which the third and fourth fingers fall furthest apart when open.

Independence (of Thought).—Hands in which the first and second fingers fall furthest apart when held loosely open.

Indigestion.—A very poorly developed narrow Cerebral and Hepatica irregular.

Infirmity (Hereditary).—The Vital interrupted in both hands and marked by small indentations. *See* **Complaints** and **Diseases.**

Ingenuity.—The Mount of ☿ prominent with square fingers and thumbs low set in the hand.

Inheritance.—An acute angle on the Rascette. If a cross or star is found near the angle great riches will accrue.

Many transverse lines on the third phalange of the finger of ♄, if the second phalange is smooth.

The Cerebral followed by a sister line. This line is seldom found. *See* **Riches;** and Diagram 1.

Inquisitiveness. — Excessively long tapering fingers and short nails.

Insanity. *See* **Madness.**

Instability. *See* **Unreliability.**

Intellect.—A good Cerebral with the Mount of ☉ developed and large thumbs.

Intellect (Weakness of at the Close of Life). The Vital bi-forked at its termination. With prudence and care this calamity may be averted, as it is generally the result of over-work.

Intelligence.—One well-marked line from the root of the finger of ☿ entering the third phalange of this finger. *See* Diagram 8.

Intelligence (Want of).—The Cerebral lying far from the Vital.

Intemperance.—The line of Mars in both hands. *See* **Ebriety.**

Intrigue.—Two lines from the Mount of ♀ to that of ♂ is a sign that two love affairs are being carried on at the same time and may lead to trouble. A star connected with either of these lines would signify an unfortunate termination.

Intrigue (Fatal). — Two lines joining the Saturnian low down in the palm of the hand, one line rising from the Mount of ♀ the other from that of ☽. This will inevitably prove disastrous unless the Saturnian promises good fortune.

Intuition.—The Cerebral, Saturnian and Mensal forming a clear triangle.

The Saturnian rising from the Mount of ☽ with the fingers of ♃ and ☉ long and tapering.

A triangle on the Mount of ☽.

A line rising on the Mount of ☽ and proceeding in a semi-circle to the Mount of ☿. *See* Diagram 10.

Irreligion. *See* **Scepticism and Ungodliness.**

J.

Jealousy.—The Mensal extending round the percussion of the hand, and the Mount of ♀ very prominent.

A long Mensal with the Mount of ☽ raised and much lined, and the Ring of Venus. *See* Diagram 3.

The Mount of ♃ completely encircled by the Mensal. *See* Diagram 4.

Judgment (Good).—A long, straight, and well-defined Cerebral extending to the Mount of ♂. *See* Diagram 8.

Judgment (Quick).—Short, smooth hands without protruding joints, or a hand in which the palm and fingers are of equal length, with the fingers square.

Justice (Sense of).—The Quadrangle regular, wide, well traced, and larger near the percussion of the hand. *See* Diagram 8.

Knotted hands with square fingers.

L.

Labour (Love of).—The Mounts of ☿ and ♂ pronounced.

A firm hand with spatulate fingers, with the second phalange of ☿ relatively long.

Law. *See* Success in.

Laziness.—The Cerebral short with the Mount of ♃ low and those of ♀ and ☽ unduly large.

The Second Angle broad and feeble.

A soft, limp hand with pointed fingers and the palm very flat in both hands.

The Mounts of ♃ and ♂ very flat.

Legacies.—Branches ascending on either side of the Vital towards the Cerebral and the Mount of ♄ or ☉. *See* Diagram 7.

A line starting from a star on the Mount of ♀ and proceeding uninterrupted to the Mount of ☉.

An angle or cross on any of the bracelets.

The Cerebral followed by a sister line. *See* Diagram 1.

Lines on the outside of the thumb's first phalange at the side near the first joint. *See* Diagram 7.

One deep line well traced on the Mount of ☉. *See* **Riches.**

Lethargy.—The Triangle very low in both hands, with a thick and short Mensal.

The Plain of Mars low, with the Mount of ☽ much raised, and a single uncrossed Bracelet well traced.

Life (Blighted).—The Saturnian broken and ending abruptly on the Plain of Mars. Diagram 2.

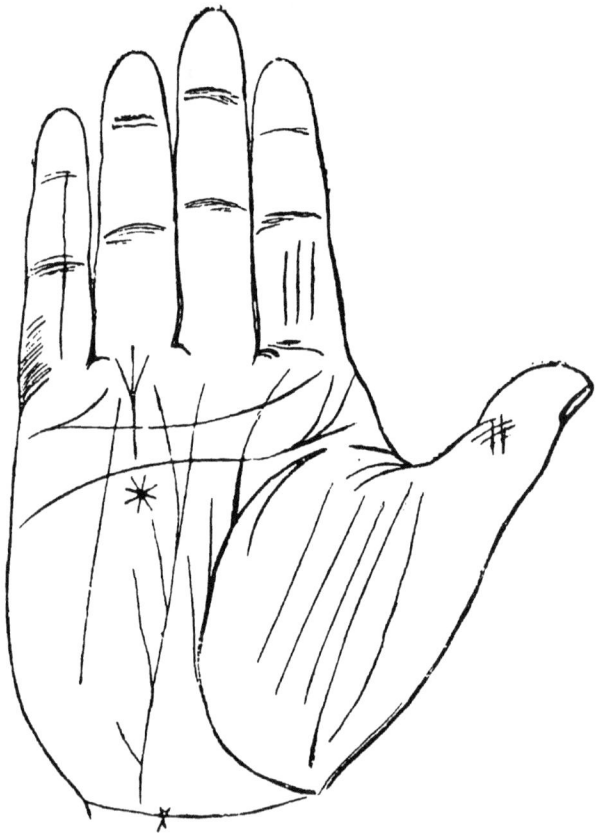

Diagram 7

A Wealthy Hand.

Life (Harassed).—Waving lines on the finger of ♄ with cross rays on the Mount.

Life (influenced by Others).—A line from the wrist extending to the Cerebral or Mensal.

A sister line following the Saturnian for a short distance.

Lines rising from the Cerebral and extending to the Mensal without actually touching it.   *See* Diagram 3.

Well formed crosses in the Quadrangle which neither cut the Saturnian or Solar denote that the subject will be under the beneficial influence of another.   If badly formed the influence would be unfavourable.   Should the branches of the cross touch the Cerebral and Mensal the influence will be lasting.

Attendant lines in the vicinity of the Vital. According to their clearness and position the extent of their influence will be shown.

Life (influenced greatly by the opposite Sex). —Lines falling from the Mensal to the Cerebral without attaching themselves.

One clear, distinct line from the Mount of ♀ to the Plain of Mars, with a star in the Quadrangle.

A star on the Mount of ♀ points to the unfortunate influence of the opposite sex.   *See* Diagram a

The influence of the opposite sex will prove fatal

when the Saturnian divides into two branches, one extending toward the Mount of ♀ the other to the Mount of ♂.

Life (Insignificant).—The Mount of ♄ very low and the Plain of Mars flat in both hands.

Entire absence of the Saturnian.

The Mount of ☿ very low in both hands, and the Vital ending in a series of crosses.

Life (Laborious).—The Rascette chained.

The Saturnian rising from the Cerebral and circling toward the Mount of ♄.

Life (Loveless).—The Vital and Mensal lying far apart, and both branchless. *See* Diagram 8.

Life (Monastic or Secluded).—A square on the Mount of ♀. *See* Diagram 2.

Life (Prosperous, Resulting from Merit.)— The Saturnian rising from the wrist and extending to the centre of the finger of ♄ in one hand only. If in both, the meaning would be different.

Life (Short).—The Cerebral terminating at the Saturnian without crossing the Fate line. *See* **Death.**

Life (Tranquil).—The Saturnian well traced and running up without interruption between the first and second fingers

Life (Unrestful when Old).—Tortuous lines at the termination of the Saturnian, giving it a confused appearance.

Logic.—Smooth hands with square fingers and the knots of philosophy pronounced.

A triangle on the Mount of ☽ with the second phalange of the thumb long and broad. *See* **Reason.**

Longevity.—A well-formed triple Bracelet with Hepatica disconnected from the Vital.

The Triangle clearly traced and well formed with an angle on one of the bracelets.

The Vital of a healthy colour, and completely encircling the thumb.

The Third Angle broad and clear, and Hepatica ascending to the Mount of ☿.

Loquacity.—The Cerebral and Mensal poorly developed, with a small Triangle at the Vital's termination, and the Mount of ☿ raised.

Love (Ardour in).—Hepatica, accompanied by " The Milky Way."

The Mensal well coloured and long, with the Mounts of ♀ and ♂ raised.

Love (Attachments of a Deep Nature).— Horizontal lines lying at the percussion of the hand between the Mensal and the finger of ☿. *See* Diagram 6.

Love (Conquests in).—The Mensal dotted with white flecks.

Love (Desire for).—Smooth fingers, with the third phalanges pointed and the Mount of ♀ raised.

Love (Devotion, Great in).—A double Mensal indicates capacity for deep devotion, which will probably lead to sorrow.

Large thumbs, the first and third phalanges being strongly developed, and firm hands.

Love (Fatal).—A cross on the Mount of ♀, unless there should be a corresponding one on the Mount of ♃. *See* Diagram 5.

The Cerebral slanting downwards and running very close to the Vital.

Lines rising from the Mount of ♀, and proceeding across the Vital, cutting both Cerebral and Mensal. Such love will make a total wreck of life. *See* Diagram 5.

Three stars in close proximity to the Vital, being posited on the outer side of the Mount of ♀. This will cause the subject to be greatly loved, but to his or her own sorrow.

The Cerebral, after traversing the hand, recoiling and running toward the Mount of ♀.

A line from the Mount of ♀ with a cross on it, indicates disaster in love by what is generally termed "falling between two stools."

Love for Near Relatives. — The marriage lines formed as islands.

Love for a Married Person.—An island on the Saturnian in both hands. Should the island be accompánied by another on the Mensal this love would stop at nothing,

Love (Happiness in).—The Line of ♂ in a woman's hand.

A star on the Mount of ♃.

The Saturnian rising from the Mount of ☽, and proceeding in a clear uninterrupted line to the Mount of ♄ without cutting the root of this finger. *See* Diagram 6.

Love (Ideal).—The longer the Mensal, and the higher it rises upon the Mount of ♃, the more ideal will the love be.

Love (Material). — The Mensal commencing under the Mount of ♄, with the Mount of ♀ strongly developed. *See* Diagram 3.

A line proceeding from the Mount of ♀ to that of ☿ or ♂, with a pale, wide Mensal.

Love (Not ending in Marriage).—Short lines ascending from the Saturnian to the Mensal.

Love (One, only for).—The Mensal evenly forked on the Mount of ♃, with a cross on the Mount of ♀.

The Saturnian losing itself in the Mensal, which then proceeds direct to the Mount of ♃.

Love (Prudence in).—A triangle on the Mount of ♀, with the second phalange of the thumb well developed

Love (Rupture with One Loved). — The Saturnian broken when near the Mensal. If the Saturnian should be broken under the Mount of ♄ the mischief will have been mere fatality, if under the Mount of ☉ pride or folly will have caused it, and if under ☿ avarice will be answerable.

Love (Skill in).—A line rising from the Mount of ♀, and proceeding in a clear, uninterrupted course to that of ☿. When this is seen in a well-endowed hand it indicates prudence and wisdom in love, but in a bad hand strategy and deceit. *See* Diagram 6.

Love (Troubles in).—The Saturnian chained when traversing the Mensal, or stopping beneath it.

The Mensal crossed by many small lines or indented.

A badly-formed star standing alone in the centre of the palm, or in the Plain of Mars. *See* **Unhappiness.**

Love (Unlawful).—An island on the Mensal.

An island stretching from the Mount of ♀ to the Mensal.

Luxuriousness.—The hands smooth, with very spatulate fingers ; and the Mounts of ♀ and ☽ much raised.

Lying.—The Cerebral bi-forked at its termination, with one branch descending to the Mount of ☽. *See* Diagram 9.

The Quadrangle very narrow in both hands, and the Mount of ☿ raised. *See* **Falsehood.**

M.

Madness.—Cerebral sloping abruptly to the Mount of ☽ and a star on the finger of ♃.

The Mount of ☽ much lined, with a star near the wrist at the Cerebral's termination.

A line from the Cerebral rising to the Mount of ♃ and joined by the Saturnian.

Madness (Danger of).—The Cerebral broken under the Mount of ♄ and sloping toward the Mount of ☽, this Mount being very prominent.

Broken or curved lines on a sloping Cerebral.

Madness (Hereditary).—A branch from the Mensal extending to the Mount of ☽ and terminating in a star.

Magic (Fatal Talent for).—A star on the first phalange of the finger of ♄, and this finger spatulate at the tip. *See* Diagram 2.

Magic (Power of).—A Triangle on the Mount of ♄, and this mount raised in both hands.

Maladies. *See* **Complaints** and **Diseases.**

Malevolence.—A grill on the Mount of ♀.

Marriage.—A long deep line cutting the percus sion of the hand on the Mount of ☿. *See* Diagram 6.

Marriage (Artist, with).—A branch from the line of marriage proceeding towards the Mount of ☉.

Marriage (with Artist). — A line from the Rascette proceeding to a branch upon the Mount of ♀ and from thence to that of ☉.

Marriage (Happy).—Saturnian rising from the Mount of ☽ and stopping at the Mensal, with a well-marked cross on the Mount of ♃.

Marriage (Lawsuits connected with). — A sharp, deep line proceeding toward the marriage line without cutting it. *See* Diagram 8.

Marriage (Prevented by Death).—A sudden sharp break in the marriage line.

Marriage (Separation Resulting In).—A line rising from the Mount of ♀ to the Mensal where it terminates in a fork.

Marriage (Unhappy).—A line rising near a star on the Mount of ☿ and running toward the Mount of ♄. *See* Diagram 8.

Cross bars on the Mount of ♄ with an island on the marriage line.

Marriage (Unsuitable).—Loss of position is shown when the marriage line cuts the Solar.

Marriage (Wealthy).—A cross and star on the Mount of ♃

A ⸂tarting from the Rascette and running tc the Mount of ♀ and from thence to that of ♃.

Marriage (with Business Man).—A line start-ing from the Rascette to the Mount of ♀ and from thence to the Mount of ☿.

Marriage (with An Old Person).—A line rising from the Rascette to the Mount of ♀ and from thence to that of ♄.

Materialism.—A cross on the third phalange of the finger of ♃. *See* Diagram 3.

A heavy pale Triangle with a large broad palm, a short thumb and thick set fingers, the third phalanges being much developed.

Meanness.—The Quadrangle and Triangle very narrow and badly formed.

The Mounts of ♃, ♀, and ☉ very flat with a poor Mensal.

Medical Skill.—The Mount of ☿ well developed with two or three well-cut lines ascending it.

Mediocrity.—A Cerebral only extending half way across the palm and a short thumb.

The Mounts of ♃, ☉, and ☿ low.

Melancholy.—The finger of ♄ very square and the first phalange broad and long.

The Mount of ☽ unduly developed with a grill, accompanied by a long, narrow, slender Vital.

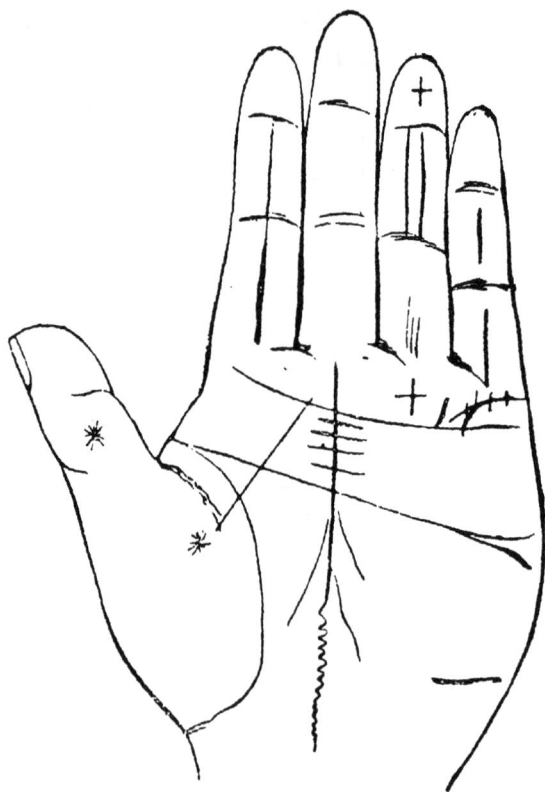

Unhappy Marriage & Childhood.
A Noble Character.

The Mount of ♄ much larger in proportion than the others.

Memory (Good).—The Cerebral extending right across the palm with Hepatica long, narrow, clear and straight.

Memory (Loss of).—The Cerebral broken up into small sections so as to give the appearance of small squares.

Military Renown.—A Triangle on the Plain of Mars between the Saturnian and the Vital.

Military Skill.—One deep line on the third phalange of the finger of ♄ and the Mount of ♂ well developed.

Mimicry.—The Cerebral ascending the Mount of ☿ at its termination.

Misfortune.—The Vital, Cerebral and Mensal all connected together at their commencement. *See* **Unhappiness** and **Troubles.**

Money. *See* **Wealth.**

Murder (Tendency to Commit).—A star on the Mount of ♂.

A dark bluish spot on the Cerebral where it traverses the Plain of Mars, the Mounts of ♂ being much raised.

N.

Naiveté.—A short thumb and tapering fingers.

Narrow-Minded.—A short Cerebral only extending to the Saturnian with the Quadrangle narrow and
the Mount of ♀ large.   *See* Diagram 9.

Excessively smooth hands with square fingers, the
Mensal   descending   toward   the   Cerebral.   *See*
Diagram 9.

The Mounts of ♃ and ♂ unduly developed with
a poor Mensal and Cerebral.

Nature (Love of).—The finger of ☋ tapering
with the others either spatulate or square.

Neatness.—Large square hands with the knot of
Order pronounced.

Nervousness.—The hand intersected by numerous
lines so as to give a confused entangled appearance.

A sister line accompanying the Vital.   *See* Diagram I.

The Mount of ☽ raised and covered with lines.

The first phalange of all the fingers inclining backwards, and the third phalanges inclining downward
below their Mounts.

Neuralgia.—An island   on   the   Cerebral.   *See*
Headaches.

Nobility of Character.—A single line on the finger of ♃ extending from the root to the first phalange. *See* Diagram 8.

The Triangle very large. *See* Diagram 8.

Nursing (Talent for).—Two clear-cut lines on the finger of ☿ .

O.

Obedience (Dutiful).—Smooth hands with square phalanges and a small palm with a square thumb.

Obstinacy.—The Cerebral commencing under the Mount of ♄ and sloping toward that of ☽ with a poor Mensal, and the finger nails wider than they are long. *See* Diagram 9.

A short weak thumb wide and heavy at the point, the first phalange being stiff and straight, with the upper knot of all the fingers developed. *See* Diagram 9.

Hard stiff hands which have a difficulty in expanding to their full extent.

Occultism (Aptitude for).—The finger of ☿ pointed with a triangle on the Mount of ☽ .

A cross in the Quadrangle beneath the finger of ♄ with a clear straight Line of Luna.

The Line of Luna forming a triangle with the Saturnian and Cerebral.

Occultism (Fatal in its Effects).—The finger of ♃ spatulate in both hands, with a cross on the Mount of ♄.

Occultism (Talent for).—A triangle on the Mount of ☽.

King Solomon's Ring in either hand.

Hepatica and Cerebral forming a clear decided cross in both hands.

A triangle on the Mount or finger of ♄.

The Cerebral descending low on to the Mount of ☽, with the second phalange of the finger of ♃ much lined.

Opportunities (Favourable).—The Saturnian rising from the Plain of Mars in both hands, if well traced, offers favourable opportunities, to be obtained only by labour and struggle.

The Saturnian well formed and rising from the Cerebral to the Mount of ♄, but to bear this signification the Cerebral must be clear and well traced, or starting from the Quadrangle and terminating beneath the finger of ♃ or ♄.

Order.—Knotted hands with large protruding joints. When the upper knots are most developed order in theory is shown, if the lower in practice.

Originality.—The Mount of ☿ highly developed,

with a long and narrow Cerebral, the fingers falling wide apart when the hands are held loosely open.

Ostentation (Love of).—The third phalange of ⊙ very long. Diagram 7.

P

Passion (Blind and Fatal).—The Cerebral rising from the side of the hand close to the Vital, and mounting toward the Mensal under the Mount of ♄, then descending again and proceeding in the usual direction.

The Mensal strongly developed and united to the Cerebral or Vital at its starting, with the Cerebral terminating in a fork, one branch of which descends to the Mount of ☽, while the other continues its natural course or joins the Mensal. *See* Diagram 4.

Passion (Capacity for Strong).—The Mount of ♀ largely developed. *See* Diagram 3.

Passion (Violent).—One deep line starting from the base of the Mount of ♀ and joining the Saturnian. Should another line from the Mount of ☽ also proceed to the Line of Fate, and attach itself in the same manner as the first, happiness may result from capricious ungoverned passion, but not till great obstacles have been encountered.

Paralysis.—All the lines on the palm feebly marked with a poor Hepatica. *See* Diseases.

Paralysis (Death by).—A Star on the Mount of ♄. *See* Diagram 10.

Two stars, one at the termination of the Vital, the other at that of the Saturnian.

Parent (Loss of a).—A small island or triangle at the commencement of the Saturnian. Diagram 2.

Pecuniary Troubles.—Lines starting from the base of the thumb and crossing the Mount of ♀ to the Cerebral. *See* Diagram 2.

Branches falling down on either side of the Vital or the Saturnian toward the wrist.

Crosses or chains on the Saturnian, unless these should happen to appear at the junction of the Saturnian with the Mensal.

Perception (Quick).—The Mount of ☿ raised with knotted hands and pointed fingers.

A spatulate hand with a short thumb, the second phalange being well developed and the finger of ♃ pointed.

Perfection (Love of).—A strong and long first phalange of the thumb.

Perfidy.—The Mount of ☿ largely developed, with the Cerebral long, thin, and poorly marked.

Perseverance.—The Mount of ♃ raised with a

good Mensal, and the thumb long, with the Cerebral extending right across the hand.

The finger of ☿ very long, and the third phalange particularly so.

A medium-sized hand, rather large than otherwise, with developed finger-knots, the outer phalanges having a square appearance.

Perspicacity.—The finger of ☿ tapering and traversed by lines, with a forked Cerebral. *See* Diagram 9.

Philosophy.—A hand with a medium-sized palm and large thumb, the phalanges of which are of equal length; knotted fingers square at their tips.

Poetry (Love of).—The Mount of ☽ raised, with a long and sloping Cerebral.

Smooth hands, with tapering fingers.

Poetry (Talent for).—Smooth fingers with small thumbs, and a grill on the Mount of ☽.

Politics (Taste for).—A triangle on the Mount of ☿. *See* Diagram 1.

Positivism.—The Mount of ☽ very flat with the Cerebral extending across the palm in a clear straight line.

The finger of ☉ square. *See* Diagram 9.

Power (Desire for).—The first phalange of the thumb strong, with a long little finger.

Practical.—Fingers square at their tips and the

same length as the palm, with the Mount of ♄ much raised.

Presence of Mind.—The Mount of ♂ under Jupiter very full.

A long, straight well-defined Cerebral, terminating on the Mount of ♂.

Presentiments.—The Mount of ☽ rayed and a circle formed by a line starting from the Mount of ☽ and proceeding to that of ☿. *See* Diagram 10.

Pride.—The Mount of ♃ well developed with a grill.

A branch from the Cerebral rising to the root of the finger of ♃.

Pride (Fatal).—A star on the Mount of ♄. *See* Diagram 10.

A branch from the Vital or Cerebral proceeding to the Mount of ♃ and there terminating in a star. The Cerebral will be short in such a hand.

Pride (Noble).—The Mount of ♂ beneath the finger of ☿ very full.

The finger of ♃ relatively long, especially the third phalange. *See* Diagram 4.

Profligacy.—One star on the outside of the thumb near the nail.

Cross bars on the Mount of ♀, unless the Mensal and Cerebral are well traced.

A star on the third phalange of the finger of ♃. *See* Diagram 3.

A triangle on the third phalange of the finger of ♄ Diagram 3.

Many crosses or lines at the root of the thumb. *See* Diagram 3.

Prudence.—The Mount of ♄ well developed.

Spatulate fingers with the knots prominent, or knotted hands with tapering fingers.

The finger of ♄ square with a straight thumb, and the second phalange full.

The Cerebral and Vital uniting to form an acute angle. Diagram 8.

Pusillanimity.—The Mount of ♂ flat in the hand and the third phalange of all the fingers inclining down below their mounts. *See* **Cowardice.**

R.

Reading (Love of).—The finger of ♃ long and tapering with the Mount of ♄ and ☉ raised, and the Cerebral good.

Realism.—Spatulate hands with strong thumbs.

Reason (Good).—Short knotted hands with large joints, the palm and fingers being of equal length, and the second phalanges of fingers being particularly long.

A triangle on the Mount of ☽.

Reason (In Art).—The second phalange of the finger of ☉ relatively longer than the others. *See* Diagram 8.

Reason (Subservient to the Heart).—A branch at the termination of the Cerebral rising and losing itself in the Mensal.

Ramifications from the Cerebral extending to the Mount of ♀.

Recklessness.—The finger of ♄ pointed with the mount flat. *See* Diagram 9.

Rectitude.—One deep line in the centre of the finger of ☿. *See* Diagram 8.

Refinement.—The Mounts of ☽ and ♀ raised with a knotted hand and pointed fingers.

Reflection.—The finger of ♃ relatively long and tapering, with the others in opposition.

The second phalanges of all the fingers larger than the others. *See* Diagram 5.

Knotted fingers, with the outer phalanges square and the joints developed.

Religion (Reverence for).—The Mount of ♃ well developed, with the first phalange of this finger relatively long.

A cross in the quadrangle. If this cross is attached to the Saturnian with smooth fingers the

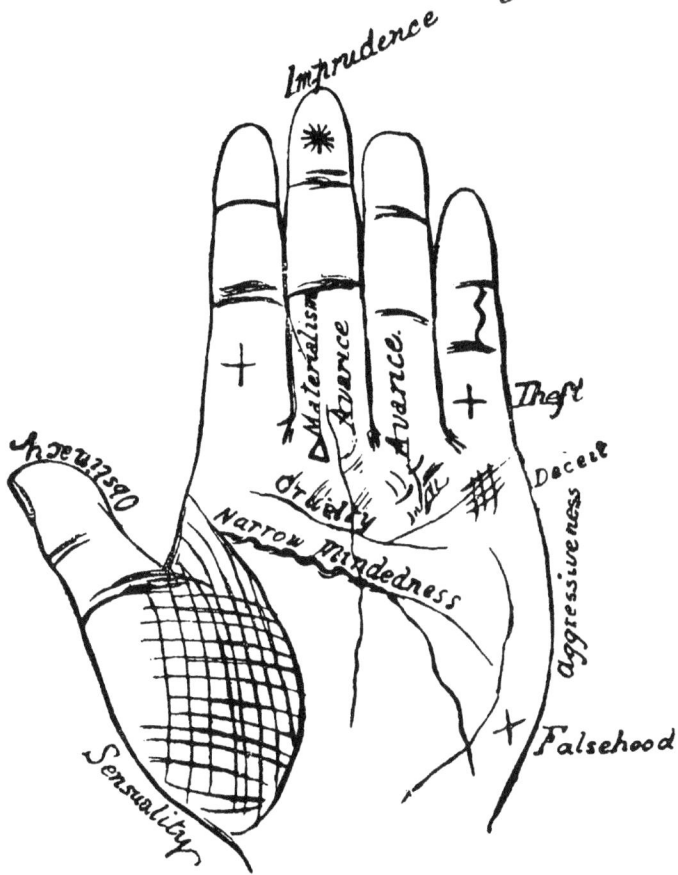

Diagram 9

Imprudence

Openness

Materialism

Avarice

Avarice

Cruelty

Will

Theft

Deceit

Narrow Mindedness

Aggressiveness

Sensuality

Falsehood

An Ignoble Character.

first phalanges being long and well developed, much consolation will be derived from religious faith.

Religion (Tolerance in).—The Mount of ☉ much raised and the finger of ♃ square with a broad quadrangle.

Resignation.—The Mount of ☽ and ♂ full but smooth without being crossed or rayed.

Resolution.—The Mount of ♂ under Jupiter raised with strong thumbs.

Restlessness.—A large palm and hard hand, with the Mounts of ♂ much lined.

Fingers longer than the palm, that of ☉ being spatulate in both hands.

Reverses.—A cross on the Mount of ☉, the Saturnian throwing off branches to the Rascette. *See* Diagram 2,

Reverses (From Woman's Influence).—Several lines rising from the root of the finger of ☉ and cutting the joints to the first phalange.

The Ring of Venus well formed, but cut by a deep bar beneath the Mount of ☉. *See* **Pecuniary Difficulties.**

Rheumatism.—The Vital biforked at the wrist, with one branch proceeding to the Mount of ☽.

Riches.—Three or more branches rising from the Cerebral to the Mount of ♃.

The Solar long and uncrossed. *See* Diagram 7.

Lines on the third phalange of the finger of ♃, with branches from the Vital ascending upwards. *See* Diagram 7.

The Mount of ☉ well developed, with two well cut lines on it.

A branch from the Cerebral extending to the Mount of ☉ with a good Saturnian. *See* Diagram 7.

A line from the Rascette crossing the Plain of Mars and terminating on the Mount of ☉. *See* **Wealth.**

Robbery.—An island on Hepatica with an unduly developed Mount of ☿. *See* **Theft.**

Romance. — The Mounts of ♀ and ☽ much raised, with a well developed Mensal.

Ruse.—One deep tortuous line cutting the finger of ☿ from the third to the second phalange. *See* Diagram 9.

S.

Savoir Faire.—The Cerebral terminating in a fork, with the absence of the Mensal. This also indicates egotism.

The Cerebral at its termination ascending toward the Mount of ☿. *See* **Tact.**

Scepticism.—A cross in the Plain of Mars under

the finger of ♄ in a hand with long fingers and the Knots of Philosophy developed.

Science (Aptitude for).—Long narrow fingers with square tips, and the finger of ☿ relatively longer than the rest.

The Mount of ☿ well developed.

The second phalange of the finger of ☿ long with the Knot of Philosophy developed.

Science (Reason in).—The finger of ☿ very square in both hands.

Science (Success in).—A triangle, or white flecks found on the Cerebral close to the Mount of ☿.

A line extending from the root to the first phalange of the finger of ☿. *See* Diagram 7.

Second-Sight. *See* **Clairvoyance and Presentiment.**

Self-Assertion.—The Cerebral and Vital entirely disconnected in both hands, with the Mounts of ♄ and ♂ unduly large.

Cross bars on the Mount of ♃, this mount being strongly developed.

Self-Confidence. *See* **Assurance.**

Self-Consciousness.—Cerebral rising toward the Mensal. *See* Diagram 10.

Self-Control.—The Mount of ♂ under ☿ large, with the first phalange of the thumb flat and inclining outwards.

Self-Deception.—A cross on the Mount of ☽, with fingers that curve backwards.

The Mensal separating into two branches, one ascending the Mount of ♄, the other descending toward the Cerebral.

Self-Esteem.—The skin of both hands very thick.

Self-Indulgence.—Very pointed fingers, shorter than the palm.

Self-Reliance.—A large space between the first and second fingers, and between the third and fourth when the hand falls loosely open.

Sensitiveness.—A large hand with the First Angle well formed but narrow, the Cerebral and Vital being closely connected with the Line of ☉ in both hands.

Sensuality.—The Ring of Venus. Should this ring open beneath the Mount of ☿ this disposition may be kept in check, unless the Mount of ♀ be much raised. *See* Diagram 3.

The Mensal taking its rise from beneath the Mount of ♄, the hands being very large, smooth and spatulate, with the third phalanges short and thick.

Sentiment.—The Saturnian dwindling to a mere thread as it nears the Vital, with the Mount of ☽ unduly large.

Shock (a Sudden).—A line from the Mount of

♀ terminating in a star or badly formed cross on the Mensal, with black flecks on the Vital or Mensal.

Sight. *See* **Blindness.**

Skill (Mechanical).—The finger of ☿ spatulate, the first phalange being relatively longer than the rest.

Somnambulism.—The Line of Luna commencing in an island.

Sorrow. *See* **Unhappiness** and **Troubles.**

Spinal Complaint.—The nails curving at the tips with the Mount of ♃ much developed.

Spirit (Want of).—The Cerebral terminating in the centre of the hand with the Mount of ♂ low.

Spirituality.—The first phalange of all the fingers very long and tapering, and the Mount of ♃ encroaching on that of ♄.

Straightforwardness. — The Quadrangle well formed, and largest near the percussion of the hand. *See* Diagram 8.

Strong-Minded. — The total absence of the Mensal, with the Mounts of ♃ and ♀ low, and that of ♂ prominent.

Subtlety.—The tip of the finger of ☿ rising above the first knot of the finger of ☉. *See* Diagram 3.

Success.—The Line of Solar in both hands.

A circle on the Mount of ☉.

The Solar rising near the Mount of ♀ and running parallel with the Vital.

Success (in Business).—The Cerebral throwing branches towards ☿ or inclining toward this mount.

The Saturnian terminating on the Mount of ☿ in both hands. *See* Diagram 3.

Success (late in Life).—The Saturnian taking its rise from the Cerebral and well marked in both hands with no cross lines barring it.

Success (Legal).—A line from the Rascette cutting the Cerebral and Mensal and proceeding to the Mount of ♃.

Success (Literary).—A cross on the upper joint of the finger of ♃. *See* Diagram 11.

A line from the wrist proceeding direct to the Mount of ☉.

A star on the Mount of ☿ accompanied by lines rising and touching the Cerebral and Mensal, with white flecks on the Cerebral beneath ☉.

Success (Military).—A triangle on the Mount of ♂.

Success (Monetary).—A branch from the Cerebral to the Solar. *See* **Riches, Wealth.**

Success (Oratorical).—A triangle on the Mount of ☿. Diagram 1.

A line running from the further extremity of the Vital to the Mount of ☿.

Success (Phenomenal).—A line from the Cerebral terminating with a star on the Mount of ♃.

Success (Theatrical).—A branch from the Saturnian proceeding to the Mount of ☿.

Suicide (Tendency to commit).—Two stars, one at the termination of the Saturnian, the other on the Mount of ☽. *See* Diagram 11.

An irregular cross on the Mount of ♂ under the finger of ☿, with the first phalange of the finger of ♄ very square and long.

The Mount of ♄ unduly large with many lines crossing the Vital and a poor Saturnian, the Cerebral being joined to Hepatica.

Superficialness.—All the phalanges of the first finger very short with the Mount of ☿ unduly developed.

Superstition.—The Mount of ♃ very prominent with a grill or cross bars.

A cross in the Quadrangle beneath the Mount of ♄ with a triangle on the mount of ♄.

The finger of ♄ very spatulate in both hands, with the first phalange well developed.

Excessively hard or soft hands with the Mount of ☽ much raised, the fingers tapering and the thumb short.

Susceptibility.—A soft hand with long fingers

and the skin much lined, the Vital being broken under the Mount of ♄.

Smooth hands with protruding joints and pointed thumbs.

T.

Tact.—Long hands with tapering fingers and fleshy balls on the inside of the first phalanges.

The finger of ☿ long and tapering. *See* Diagram 8.

The Cerebral and Mensal good with a triangle at the Vital's termination.

A total absence of the Mensal with the second phalange of the thumb wasp-shaped.

Tactlessness.—The Vital and Cerebral far removed from one another, the hands being excessively smooth and the fingers spatulate.

The Cerebral straight and the finger of ☿ very short with the knots well developed.

Talent.—Thumbs set very low on the hands.

Talent (Diplomatic).—The Cerebral forked, one branch descending to the Mount of ☽ and the Mount of ☿ well developed.

Talent (Dramatic).—The finger of ☉ spatulate in both hands.

Talent (Medical).—Three perpendicular well cut lines on the Mount of ☿. *See* Diagram 11.

Talent (as a Statesman).—The Cerebral terminating in a fork, one branch ascending to the Mount of ☿, the other sloping down to the Mount of ☽.

Teeth (Bad).—The Saturnian and Hepatica long and tortuous with the second phalanges of all the fingers relatively longer than the others. *See* Diagram 5.

Temper (Bad).—The finger-nails square at the root and of a red colour, with a short first phalange to the thumb.

The Mount of ♂ unduly developed with the Plain of Mars much lined and a cross lying in the middle.

Temper (Captious).—Two crosses on the inner side of the thumb's upper joint, with the Mount of ♂ underlying ☿ low, and that of ♂ under ♃ developed.

The Vital irregular and tortuous, with the third angle badly formed and the palm much lined.

Temper (Obstinate).—The first phalange of the thumb wide and short, the Mensal poor and the Cerebral commencing beneath ♃ and sloping on to the Mount of ☽. *See* Diagram 9.

Temper (Passionate).—The finger-nails broad and square at their roots, with hard hands and a cross in the Triangle.

The Mount of ♂ excessively developed with a grill or cross.

Tenderness.—The Mensal traversed by a small line at its termination with the Mount of ♀ raised.

Theft.—Many confused lines on the third phalange of the finger of ☿.

A cross on the third phalange of the finger of ☿. *See* Diagram 9.

A star on the Mount of ☿, and this finger spatulate in both hands.

The Mount of ☿ much developed with a cross or grill. *See* Diagram 9.

Thoughtfulness.—The finger of ♃ long and tapering with the others square. A well-defined clear Cerebral and a broad Quadrangle.

Thoughtlessness.—All the phalanges of the finger of ♃ short in both hands and the Mount low. *See* Diagram 10.

Timidity.—The Mounts of ♂ and ♄ very flat, with the Cerebral and Vital joined for a considerable distance.

A grill on the Mount of ☽ and the Quadrangle narrow, caused by the Cerebral rising toward the Mensal. *See* Diagram 10.

Fingers which are stiff and that have a natural tendency to curve inwards towards the palm.

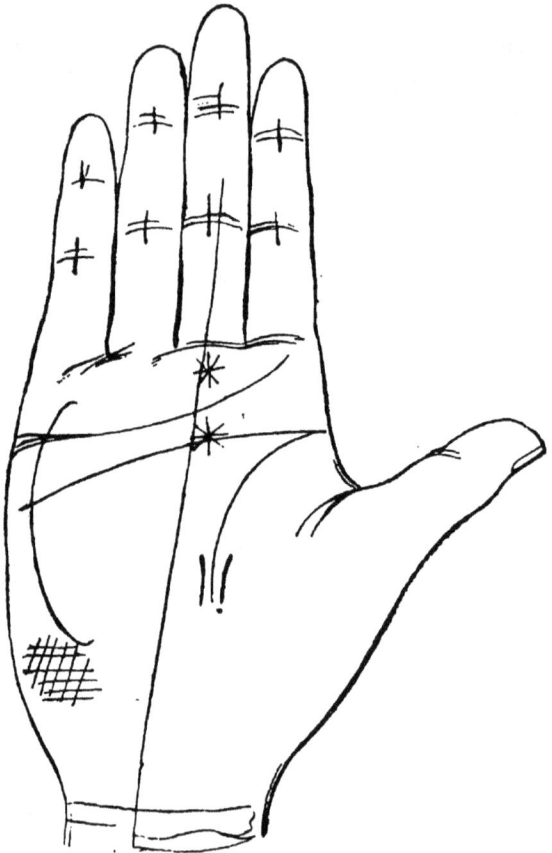

Diagram 10

Sudden Death.

Tolerance.—A high Mount of ♂, smooth as well as raised, with a broad Quadrangle, particularly large near the percussion of the hand.   Diagram 8.

Tolerance (Want of).—Large knotted hands.

Tranquility.   *See* **Life.**

Travels.—A branch from Hepatica extending to the Mount of ♃.

When the Vital separates into two branches, one circling round the Mount of ♀ and the other sloping to the Mount of ☽, a complete change to another country is imminent.

Travels (Continuous).—A branch or branches proceeding from the Rascette to the Mount of ☽.

The Saturnian rising from the Mount of ☽ and many horizontal lines barring this mount crossing the percussion of the hand.   *See* Diagram 6.

Travels (Influenced by Opposite Sex).—A branch from the Mount of ☽ running across to the Mount of ♀.

Travels (resulting in Good Fortune).—A cross at the extreme limit of the Quadrangle posited between the Mounts of ♂ and ☽.

A line rising from the Rascette and proceeding direct to the Mount of ♃.

Troubles.—The Rascette badly formed or broken. *See* Diagram 2.

Troubles (caused by Others).—A cross in the Plain of ♂ predicts troubles from strangers, and from relations if on the Mount of ♀ next the Vital.

Many lines from the Mount of ♀ cutting the Vital. Should they stop at the Cerebral money will be the trouble, if at the Mensal love will be thwarted. *See* Diagram 5.

A cross on the Mount of ☉, or on a line running towards this mount, foretells troubles connected with money.

Troubles (connected with Marriage).—The marriage line crossed by many small perpendicular lines. *See* Diagram 8.

One deep horizontal line on the Mount of ☽, with a star on the Mount of ♀. *See* Diagram 8.

The Vital, Cerebral, Mensal and marriage line cut by a line starting from the Mount of ☿.

Troubles (from Death or Unfaithfulness).— One deep line starting from the lower joint of the thumb across the Mount of ♀ and cutting the Vital.

A branch from the Saturnian sloping toward the Mount of ☽.

Troubles (in Middle Life).—The Saturnian poorly marked as it approaches the centre of the hand.

Troubles (from Relations).—Stars or crosses on the inside of the line drawn by the Vital, and close to it. Should the branches of these crosses touch the Life line the troubles would be of a very serious nature.

Troubles (from a Woman).—A line from the Saturnian sloping down and attaching itself to the Vital.

A circle on the Plain of Mars.

Troubles (throughout Life).—A tortuous and irregular Saturnian, with many lines cutting the Vital and Saturnian. *See* **Unhappiness**, Diagram 2.

Truthfulness.—The fingers of ☉ and ♃ square.

Knotted hands with square phalanges and tapering fingers, the finger of ♃ alone being square.

Tyranny.—Excessively long hands, with a narrow palm, and the first phalange of the thumb very long.

The Mount of ☽ very low, with that of ♂ much raised.

The Mount of ♃ strongly developed, with a grill.

A long, slender smooth hand, with stiff square fingers, and the Vital broad and of a red colour.

U

Uncertainty. *See* **Vacillation.**

Uncharitableness. — The Second Angle very

broad and heavy, with a poor Mensal and narrow Quadrangle. *See* Diagram 9.

Understanding (Dull).—One deep line traversing the entire finger of ♄. *See* Diagram 11.

The Cerebral pale and wide, the First and Third Angle very obtuse.

The Saturnian taking its rise from the Cerebral, with the Mounts of ♃, ☉ and ☿ low.

Understanding (Good).—The Mounts of ☿ and ☉ much raised, with the Vital terminating in a cross.

The Third Angle broad and well formed, with the second phalanges of all the fingers developed and longer in proportion than the rest.

The Triangle wide and clearly marked, with the lines of a good colour.

Straight, well-cut lines on the second or third phalange of the finger of ☿. *See* Diagram 8.

The finger of ☿ relatively long, and a branch rising from the Cerebral toward the Mount of ☿.

Understanding (Weak).—The Mounts of ☉, ♀, and ☽ very low in both hands, with the Triangle narrow and badly formed.

The Mensal short and thick, excessively hard hands with tapering fingers.

A large hand with a long palm and short fingers, the Quadrangle being furrowed by many lines.

Unfairness.—A narrow Quadrangle, with the Mounts of ♂ and ☿ much raised.

Unfaithfulness.—A crescent on the Triangle, and the Third Angle very obtuse.

The first phalange of the thumb insignificant and relatively short.

Ungodliness.—A low Mount of ♃ in both hands, with the first phalanges of all the fingers poorly developed.

Unhappiness.—An irregular cross in the centre of the Triangle, with cross-bars on the Mount of ♄.

A star lying beneath the Mount of ♄. *See* Diagram 10.

The Saturnian tortuous and chained with a second line clinging to it.

A semicircle described on the third phalange of the finger of ☉.

Lines rising from the wrist and traversing the Mount of ☽ toward the Line of Health (Hepatica).

Unhappiness (in Childhood).—Many small indentations or crosses at the commencement of the Vital or Saturnian. *See* Diagram 8.

Unhappiness (Misplaced Affection caused by).—Lines falling from the Saturnian to the Rascette. *See* Diagram 8.

A star on the Mount of ♀. *See* Diagram 8.

Cerebral arching toward the Mensal and then abruptly falling on to the Vital.   *See* **Love.**

The Saturnian rising from the Mount of ☽ and terminating at the Mensal.

Unhappiness (Personal Conduct caused by). —A weak Mensal with the Cerebral commencing beneath the Mount of ♄ and terminating on the Mount of ♂   The misfortune will arise from the subjects' own obstinacy, or from a mistaken calculation.

The Saturnian stopping abruptly at the Cerebral in both hands will bring misfortune owing to a mistaken view of matters unless the Saturnian be well formed, and there are other favourable signs in the hand. *See* Diagram 4.

Unhappiness   (Throughout   Life). — The Saturnian rising from below the Rascette and cutting the finger of ♄.   The higher it penetrates the worse misfortune will there be.   *See* Diagram 10.

The first Angle placed low on the hand, close to the Plain of Mars.

Unhappiness (From Woman).—A star at the base of the Mount of ♀, or just below the second phalange of the thumb.

Unreliability.—A small palm with a short thumb and the fingers broad at the third phalange with a sloping Cerebral that terminates in a fork.

Unselfishness.— The finger of ☿ very short with a well-traced Mensal, and branches rising from it.   *See* Diagram 4.

Untruth.—A cross on the Mount of ☽ and the third phalange of the little finger very long in both hands.   *See* Diagram 9.

A poor Cerebral and Mensal with a triangle at the termination of the Vital.

Transverse lines on the second phalange of the finger of ♃, or confused lines on the second phalange of the finger of ☿.

The Mount of ♄ unduly developed with a grill, and the Mount of ☉ raised.

Uprightness.—One well-marked line traversing the entire length of the finger of ☿.   *See* Diagram 7.

V.

Vacillation.—The first phalanges of the thumb very short with the second long and thick denotes indecision through excess of prudence.

The Cerebral extending half way across the palm, broad and of a pale colour.

The Quadrangle narrow owing to the ascent of the Cerebral toward the Mensal, with a spatulate hand and short thumb.

Vanity.—Cross-bars on the Mount of ☉ with the Mount of ♀ unduly large.

The third phalange of the finger of ☉ very long, with the Mount of ☉ much lined.

The Mount of ☉ flat with a grill, and the Vital bi-furcated at its commencement.

Vanity (Overwhelming).—A branch from the Cerebral mounting high on to the Mount of ♃ to the root of the finger, and then recoiling toward the Mount of ♄.

Versatility.—Mixed hands with supple fingers.

Vindictiveness.—A narrow Quadrangle with a long Cerebral and poor Mensal, the Mounts of ♂ and ♃ being much raised. Diagram 9.

Vivacity.—The absence of Hepatica with the Mount of ☿ much developed.

Small soft supple hands with pronounced joints.

Voluptuousness. *See* **Profligacy.**

Voyages.—Hepatica taking its course across the Mount of ☽, and proceeding along the percussion of the hand. Diagram 5.

Lines descending from the Mount of ☽ to the wrist, or rising from the Rascette to the Mount of the moon.

The Line of Intuition found in both hands and crossed by many small lines inclining toward the Vital or Saturnian.

Voyages (Long).—A line starting from the Bracelets and proceeding toward the Mount of ♃, with a horizontal bar on the Mount of ☽.

The Vital separating into two branches, one of these proceeding toward the Mount of ☽.

Voyages (Lucky).—A cross posited between the Mount of ☽ and the Triangle, or in the Quadrangle by the Mount of ♂.

W.

Wealth.—Branches from the Saturnian or Vital, rising towards the Mount of ☉.   *See* Diagram 7.

Several lines with a star on the Mount of ☉.

The Cerebral followed by a sister line.   *See* Diagram 1.

Cross lines at the side of the first phalange of the thumb, with the Line of Solar in both hands.   *See* Diagram 7.

The Triple Bracelet well marked with a branch from Hepatica mounting toward ☉.

The Line of Mars in both hands, with transverse lines on the third phalange of the first finger.

The Solar narrow, deep and straight, ascending the Mount of ☉ uncrossed in both hands.   Diagram 7.

Diagram XI

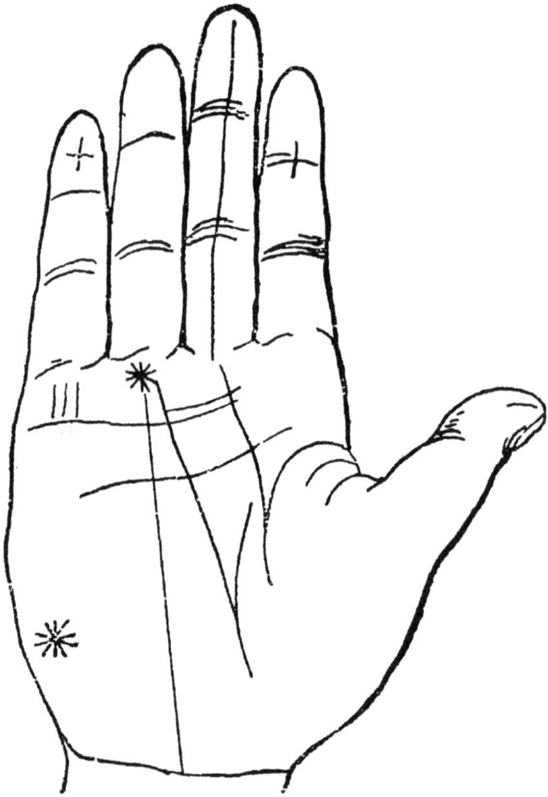

A Very Serious Illness

Straight, well-cut lines on the Mount of ♄ or on the Mount of ☿, with a star in the Triangle.

An angle or cross on the upper Bracelet and a line from the Cerebral to the Mount of ♃.

A branch or branches rising from the Vital to the Cerebral, and after crossing the Mensal terminating on the Mount of ♃ or ☉. *See* Diagram 7.

Wealth (Acquired).—Well-marked lines on the Mount of ☉, if uncrossed and seen in both hands.

Wealth (Fatal to Happiness).—A star on the Mount of ☉ when the Solar is wanting in both hands.

Wealth (Late in Life).—Two branches proceeding from the Rascette to the Mount of ☉.

Branches from the Vital sloping toward the Plain of Mars, with a good Saturnian.

Wealth (Unexpected).—A cross on any of the bracelets.

Wickedness.—A Triangle on the Mount of ♄, accompanied by a star on the first phalange of the finger. *See* Diagram 9.

Widowhood.—The Line of Marriage sloping down toward the Mensal.

A line extending from the Mensal to the Saturnian with an interrupted Line of Fate.

A black fleck on the Line of Marriage.

Will (Firm).—The first phalange of the thumb strongly developed, with the finger of ☿ long. Diagram 8.

A long, straight well-defined Cerebral, and the Mounts of ♂ and ♃ well developed.

Will (Weak).—A short Cerebral, and the first phalange of the thumb poor and weak.

Wisdom.—The Mounts of ♄ and ☉ well developed.

A line from the third phalange of the finger of ☉ cutting the second phalange very deeply. *See* Diagram 1.

One or two lines extending from the third to the second phalange of the finger of ♄.

Wit.—The Mount of ☿ well developed, and the First Angle well cut and narrow.

The Ring of Venus. *See* Diagram 3.

Women (Fatal Influence of).—A crescent on the Mount of ☾.

Women (Influence of).—A well-formed star in the Quadrangle shows that a man is both good and true, but liable to be at the mercy of any woman he loved.

Women (Love of).—The Line of Mars. *See* Diagram 1 and **Love (Ardour in).**

Worries.—Lines proceeding from the Plain of Mars and intersecting the Vital. *See* **Pecuniary Difficulties** and **Troubles.**

Wound (on the Head).—A star on the Cerebral. *See* Diagram 10.

Wound (Mortal).—The Cerebral broken under the Mount of ♄ in both hands, with the lines piled on each other. *See* **Accidents.**

Wound (Serious).—Lines rising from the centre of the palm and traversing the Vital to the root of the thumb.

Printed by Henry J. Drane, Ye Saint Bride's Presse, Salisbury House, Salisbury Square, London, E.C.